Under the editorship of

DAYTON D. McKEAN

University of Colorado

OTHER TITLES IN THE SERIES

✛

The Federal

Government of

Switzerland

✛

GEORGE ARTHUR CODDING, Jr.
UNIVERSITY OF COLORADO

HOUGHTON MIFFLIN COMPANY · BOSTON

1965 *Impression*

The Riverside Press *Cambridge, Massachusetts*
PRINTED IN THE U.S.A.

To

MAUDE

CONTENTS

CONTENTS

PREFACE

If one were to choose a single word to describe the general impression that one receives upon entering Switzerland, that word would have to be "tranquillity." The sight of its green mountain meadows, fertile valleys, and shimmering lakes lulls the visitor and increases his sense of well being. Contact with the people and their work does little or nothing to disturb this overall impression. The transportation system is efficient and orderly; the hotels and restaurants are, on the whole, gracious and quiet; the factories are remarkably neat and clean; and the people appear well fed and content.

A visit to the Federal Capitol in Berne is a lesson in tact and orderliness. The corridors of the government buildings seem to lack the noise and confusion that are distinguishing characteristics of many centers of government in the modern world. In the offices themselves, government personnel conscientiously carry out their assigned tasks with a minimum of fuss and publicity. The meetings of the federal legislature, even when an important piece of legislation is under consideration, are singularly free of bombast and raised tempers.

Compared to the history of many of its neighbors, that of Switzerland is remarkably lacking in violence and conflict. Although the revolutions that shook Europe in the eighteenth and nineteenth centuries had their repercussions in Switzerland, they did not foment the same violent upheavals and the almost complete break with the past that occurred elsewhere. Switzerland was also able to remain officially aloof from the two major wars of the twentieth century. Although Switzerland mobilized her manpower and stood guard on her frontiers, her standard of living was not greatly affected, nor were her cities ravaged by enemy action.

Switzerland has not, however, allowed herself to be lulled into atrophy or forced into the backwaters of modern history. From a land whose resources are poor in the extreme, Swiss ingenuity has created a rich industrial economy. Swiss manufactured products are admired and purchased in almost every country, and the revenues from exports help provide the Swiss with one of the highest standards of living in the world. Switzerland is active in international affairs, European and world-wide, and her advice is regarded with respect. She was a spirited member of the League of Nations, the headquarters of which were in Geneva. Although Switzerland is not now a member of the United Nations, the European headquarters of the United Nations is located there, as are the headquarters of a number of Specialized Agencies of which

Switzerland is an active member. The Swiss-run International Committee of the Red Cross has an important impact throughout the world.

The purpose of this work is to investigate the Federal political institutions to which the Swiss owe so much in their struggle to create and maintain the conditions of the life they are privileged to enjoy. Although the basic approach is descriptive, it is descriptive of both theory and practice. It is important to describe the political institutions as they are set forth in the fundamental documents since one must always be aware of the machinery and the rules which lay down the general limits of action. It is also important to know how those rules and institutions are adapted to meet changing conditions, social, economic, and political.

The plan of this study is simple. After a brief survey of the land and its people and the history of Swiss constitutional development, all essential to an understanding of the *raison d'être* of the political institutions, the political institutions themselves will be examined one by one, commencing with the important practice of direct democracy. An investigation of the three major organs of government, legislative, executive, and judicial, will be followed by a chapter devoted to Swiss political parties and interest groups. There follow chapters on general domestic policies and on foreign policy and neutrality. Rather than being presented in a separate chapter, the local units of government, the cantons and communes, will be discussed throughout the study when a description is pertinent to the question at hand.

The fact that Switzerland has two major languages, French and German, creates a certain amount of confusion in the nomenclature of the cantonal units (Italian is the language of the majority only in the Canton of Ticino). In order to ward off the possibility of such a confusion forming in the reader's mind, the names of the twenty-two Swiss cantons (three of which are divided into six half-cantons) as they are used in this text along with their French and German equivalents, are listed on page xii.

This volume could never have been written without the wholehearted support and assistance of a great many people. Almost everyone the author met during his several years of residence in Switzerland helped him to a better understanding of Switzerland and the Swiss — officials of the executive branch of government, members of parliament, officials of all the major political parties, and just plain citizens. On this side of the Atlantic, the author has been fortunate in having the cooperation of the Swiss Embassy in Washington and the Swiss Consulate General in Philadelphia. The author is very much aware of his tremendous debt of gratitude to these many helpful people and hopes that they realize that it would be impossible to thank each and every one by name. The author also hopes that they will forgive him for acknowledging his special thanks to a number of personal friends. Of particular help were Dr. Tennent H. Bagley, Dr. Henry J. Abraham, Mr. Heinz K. Hinterman, Mr. Walter Skurnik, and Mrs. Nancy Masland. Of an extremely pleasant and informative nature were the many hours of political discussion over glasses of good Swiss wine with Dr. Fred Maret in Berne and Mr. F. J. Hugon in Geneva. A very special debt of gratitude is owed to Miss Yolanda C. Legnini for her help in all stages of the manuscript. Finally, thanks are due to the editorial staff of Houghton Mifflin Company. The author, of course, assumes responsibility for any inaccuracies or errors that remain.

NAMES OF THE SWISS CANTONS

As used in this text	French	German
1. Appenzell	Appenzell	Appenzell
a. Inner Rhodes	a. Rhodes Intérieures	a. Inner Rhoden
b. Outer Rhodes	b. Rhodes Extérieures	b. Ausser Rhoden
2. Aargau	Argovie	Aargau
3. Basle	Bâle	Basel
a. Basle Town	a. Bâle-Ville	a. Basel-Stadt
b. Basle Country	b. Bâle-Campagne	b. Basel-Land
4. Berne	Berne	Bern
5. Fribourg	Fribourg	Freiburg
6. Geneva	Genève	Genf
7. Glarus	Glaris	Glarus
8. Grisons	Grisons	Graubünden
9. Lucerne	Lucerne	Luzern
10. Neuchâtel	Neuchâtel	Neuenburg
11. Schaffhausen	Schaffhouse	Schaffhausen
12. Schwyz	Schwyz	Schwyz
13. Solothurn	Soleure	Solothurn
14. St. Gallen	St-Gall	St. Gallen
15. Ticino*	Tessin	Tessin
16. Thurgau	Thurgovie	Thurgau
17. Unterwalden	Unterwald	Unterwalden
a. Nidwalden	a. Nidwald	a. Nidwalden
b. Obwalden	b. Obwald	b. Obwalden
18. Uri	Uri	Uri
19. Valais	Valais	Wallis
20. Vaud	Vaud	Waadt
21. Zurich	Zurich	Zürich
22. Zug	Zoug	Zug

*Italian usage.

$\div$ *1* $\div$

The Land and
Its People

If one were to choose a country in which to establish a modern nation-state, Switzerland would not be first choice. (Physically, it lacks direct access to the sea; it is surrounded by neighbors many times its own size; much of the soil is unproductive; and it is almost wholly lacking in essential raw materials.) From a demographic point of view, Switzerland looks just as unpromising. (The population is relatively small; it is fairly evenly divided between those who profess the Catholic and Protestant faiths; and it consists of three major language groups.)

Despite these liabilities, the Swiss have established a modern nation-state. Consequently, our first task is to examine the conditions particular to the land and its people which, of necessity, have had a decisive influence on both the form that the Swiss political institutions have taken and the manner in which these institutions have exercised their basic functions.

Geography

Switzerland is a small, landlocked country lying approximately in the center of Western Europe and surrounded by (Italy, France, Germany, and Austria in order of the extent of the common frontiers.) Its 15,941 square miles make it one of the most compact countries in Europe. If one excludes the four miniature states — Andorra, Liechtenstein, Monaco, and San Marino — Switzerland exceeds in size only Albania, Belgium, Luxembourg, and the Netherlands. The smallest of its neighbors, Austria, is slightly over two times as large.

1

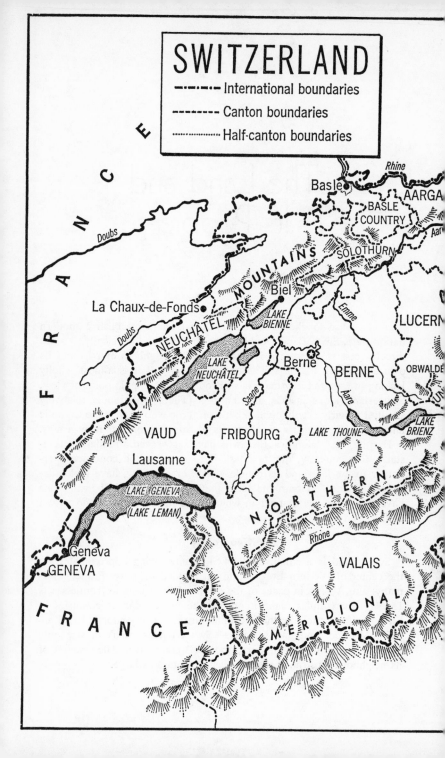

Switzerland is divided into three major regions, the Jura, the Plateau, and the Alps. The Jura mountains to the northwest comprise 10 per cent of the surface of the country. The exact limits of the Plateau in the center and the Alps in the south are more difficult to determine because of the intrusion of the Alpine foothills. However, if one considers that the southern frontier of the Plateau passes through the towns of Vevey, Thoune, Lucerne, St. Gallen, and Rorschach, the Plateau makes up approximately 30 per cent of the country and the Alps the remaining 60 per cent.

The Swiss Alps can be represented as forming three parallel waves whose crests are oriented from the southwest to the northeast and which are comprised of the Préalps, or foothills of the Alps, the Northern Alps, and the Meridional Alps. The Préalps rise from the Plateau and reach toward the northern Alps to the south. The Northern Alps are separated from the higher Meridional Alps by the valleys of the Rhone and the Rhine which form a depression running roughly from the towns of Martigny in the Valais to Chur (Coire) in the Grisons. The Northern Alps are made up of three principal chains, the Bernese Alps, the Urner Alps, and the Glarus Alps. The Meridional Alps are subdivided into the Valais Alps (Pennine Alps), the Lepontine Alps, and the Rhaetian Alps. The Alps are the watershed of Europe, providing the sources of the Rhine flowing northward to the North Sea, the Rhone flowing southwest to the Mediterranean, and the tributaries of rivers which become the Danube and the Po flowing into the Black and the Adriatic Seas, respectively.

Actually a branch of the Alps, the Jura is a limestone range lying to the northwest. Although much lower than the Alps proper, at the highest point only 5,500 feet above sea level as compared to the 15,217 feet of Alpine Monte Rosa, the Jura is broken up into a multitude of valleys and mountain ranges.

The Swiss Plateau, caught between the Jura in the North and the Alps in the south, follows the same general configuration as the mountain ranges; its limits are Lake Geneva (Lake Léman) in the southwest and Lake Constance (Bodensee) in the northeast. Never much more than twenty miles wide at any point, the Plateau is also broken into numerous subdivisions by valleys and ranges of hills. Prehistoric actions of Alpine glaciers account for the fertile soil of the Plateau and for its numerous lakes.

Aside from the compartmentalization created by the major mountain ranges and valleys and supplemented by hundreds of smaller transverse valleys, one of the major characteristics of the Swiss land is its extreme poverty. Almost 24 per cent of the total surface of Switzerland is completely unproductive, being made up of glaciers, rocky peaks, and lakes. Some 23 per cent is comprised of forests and another 23 per cent of high grassland and meadows. Only the remaining 30 per cent of the Swiss soil can be used for the raising of the necessary basic food crops. In ordinary times, Switzerland's soil can provide only about three-fifths of the foodstuffs necessary to feed her population.

In raw materials, Switzerland is a poor country indeed. With the exception of cement and building stone, none of the necessities of modern industrial production are present. There is a complete lack of any important coal, iron, petroleum, or mineral deposits. The only saving grace, but an important one, is the fact that abundant sources of electrical energy exist.

Population

The 1960 census figures place the resident population of Switzerland at 5,429,061, including approximately 582,800 foreigners. In total population, Switzerland is again a small country, exceeding only seven other European countries: Albania, Denmark, Finland, Iceland, Ireland, Luxembourg, and Norway. In density of population, however, it is high on the scale of European countries following Belgium, Germany, the United Kingdom, Italy, and the Netherlands.

The geographical distribution of the Swiss population is unequal. About two-thirds of the inhabitants live in the Plateau which, as noted earlier, comprises only about a third of the total area of the country. In 1960 well over half lived in the six largest cantons, all situated in the Plateau: Zurich (952,304), Berne (889,523), Vaud (429,512), Aargau (360,940), St. Gallen (339,489), and Geneva (259,234).[2]

Although the Swiss are flocking more and more to a few cantons, they are not necessarily large city dwellers. In 1960 there were only five cities with a population of more than 100,000: Zurich (440,170), Basle (206,746), Geneva (176,183), Berne (163,172), and Lausanne (126,328).[3] The relative preference of the Swiss to live in the country or in small towns and villages stems not only from the availability of

[1] Bureau Fédéral de Statistique, *Annuaire statistique de la Suisse,* 1963 (Basle: Editions Berkhäuser, 1963), pp. 21 and 25. All of the statistics which follow, unless otherwise designated, are taken from this publication. The population of Switzerland in 1950 was 4,714,992 including 285,446 foreigners.

[2] The six largest cantons and their population in 1950 were: Berne (801,943), Zurich (777,002), Vaud (337,585), St. Gallen (309,106), Aargau (300,782), and Lucerne (223,249).

[3] The population for the same cities in 1950 were Zurich (390,020), Basle (183,543), Berne (146,499), Geneva (145,473), and Lausanne (106,807).

transportation, which is excellent, but also from the decentralization of industry, which has a long history, including the search for water power. The urbanization movement in Switzerland is demonstrated in Table 1.

Table 1

Urbanization

Inhabitants in:	1850	1900	1950*
		(2)	(5)
Large towns (over 100,000)	None	259,864	972,342
Medium size towns between 30,000 and 100,000)	(1) 31,238	(5) 239,480	(5) 277,104
Small towns (between 10,000 and 30,000)	(7) 122,959	(14) 229,041	(32) 470,611

* The cities in the medium size category in 1950 were St. Gallen, Winterthur, Lucerne, Bienne, and La Chaux-de-Fonds.

One of the major purposes of the Constitution of 1848, which made Switzerland a federation, and the constitutional revision of 1874, was to break down rigid cantonal barriers and to create a true Swiss nationality in order to meet changing economic and social conditions. Table 2 shows how the Swiss took advantage of their freedom to migrate to those areas in Switzerland where opportunities beckoned. Probably the most important trend is that of the increasing movement of Swiss into cantons other than those of birth. The increase from 7.3 per cent to 23.6 per cent over the period of 100 years may not seem

Table 2

Place of Birth of Swiss Residents

(Percentages)

Year	Commune of Residence	Other Communes of Same Cantons	Other Cantons	Foreign Countries
1860	63.8	24.6	7.3	4.3
1888	56.5	25.6	11.5	6.4
1900	52.0	24.8	13.9	9.3
1910	48.4	24.4	15.4	11.8
1920	47.2	25.1	18.5	9.2
1930	45.2	25.0	21.0	8.8
1941	44.3	25.9	23.0	6.8
1950	43.7	24.4	23.6	8.3

significant to an American, because labor mobility in the United States has always been high. It is, however, significant in Switzerland where the size of the country is small and where loyalties to the commune and the canton of birth have always been extremely strong.

There has always been a steady movement of Swiss citizens to other parts of the world. In 1962, for instance, it was estimated that some 157,877 Swiss passport holders were registered as residents at the various Swiss diplomatic and consular missions abroad. Europe led the list with 103,980, the Americas followed with 37,953, Africa with 9,006, and Asia with 3,838. In Europe the favored countries were France, West Germany, and Italy in that order. In the Americas, most Swiss were in the United States. The Swiss who leave for foreign parts, however, do not necessarily stay away from Switzerland forever. Many work for Swiss firms in the country of residence, and very few give up their Swiss nationality, especially since Switzerland permits dual nationality. In 1962, for example, while 8,725 Swiss were registered as emigrating, 7,622 were listed as returning to Switzerland from residence abroad and only 70 were shown to have renounced their nationality.

Concomitantly Switzerland does not lack in attractions for citizens of other countries. Despite the complicated formalities involved, 1,937 foreigners were naturalized in 1961. Even without citizenship, foreigners are eager to come to Switzerland as a place to live and especially as a place to work. In 1962 alone new residence permits for workers numbered 455,753. Italians were the most numerous, Germans were second, and Austrians third. Of these, 222,459 were given work permits for seasonal work, 176,838 were for non-seasonal work, and 2,502 unclassified were restricted to a short term without renewal. Another group of 53,858 were given frontier work passes which permitted them to work in Switzerland during the day and return to their homes in neighboring countries at night. The largest number of these workers admitted in 1962 was scheduled for work in non-skilled basic occupations: construction (176,849), hotel and restaurant work (55,763), agriculture (18,845), and domestic service (15,691). Of the total, 343,585 were men and 112,168 were women. The total foreign labor force in 1960 numbered well over 500,000.

Language and Religion

Perhaps second only to the overwhelming physical beauty that abounds everywhere, the characteristic that amazes most Americans visiting in Switzerland for the first time is the linguistic diversity. Within the space of a few short miles, and within the same national frontier, one can travel through areas where the native tongue may be French, German, Italian, or Romanche, the latter being an odd language of Latin origin. The Swiss language diversity can also be a matter of confusion for the visitor. Only a compass can help some one going the few miles from Berne to Neuchâtel if he doesn't know that the latter is Neuenburg in German. The demarcation lines of the different languages take no account of cantonal boundaries, and there is little or no transition from one language to another; one small village may be exclusively French-speaking, and a neighboring village may be exclusively German-speaking. The major division, German and French, runs approximately from Delémont in the north to Bienne and Fribourg in the Plateau, passes through the Bernese Alps and crosses Valais just above Sierre in the southwest.

German is the predominant Swiss language. According to the 1960 census, excluding resident foreigners, 74.4 per cent of the Swiss are German-speaking, 20.2 per cent are French-speaking, 4.1 per cent speak Italian, and 1.0 per cent speak Romanche. Other languages make up the remaining 0.3 per cent. The proportions have not changed radically over the years. In 1910, for example, the percentages were, respectively, 72.7, 22.1, 3.9, 1.2, and 0.1. Table 3 gives the 1950 breakdown by cantons.

The Swiss Federal Constitution provides that four languages — German, French, Italian, and Romanche — are the "national" languages of Switzerland but that only German, French, and Italian are the "official" languages. The process of making a language "official" guarantees the right of a Swiss citizen to petition the government in any of those languages, permits a member of the national legislature to use them before his colleagues, and permits their use in the pleading of cases before the Federal Tribunal. Article 107 of the Constitution also provides that all three language groups must be represented on the Swiss high court. All Federal statutes and ordinances are published in French, German, and Italian. As a national but not an official language, Romanche is given status without its use being compulsory. While Switzerland is multi-lingual as a nation, the individual citizens are not necessarily so. Although a very large percentage of the Swiss speak more than one language, the French-speaking citizens are less likely to learn German than the German-speaking citizens are to learn French. Many listed as Italian-speaking prefer French to German as a second language, and most of those listed as Romanche-speaking also know German. It should also be noted that while the French and

Table 3

Languages Spoken (in 1950)

(Percentages)

Canton	German	French	Italian	Romanche	Other
Zurich	93.4	2.1	3.2	0.4	0.9
Berne	83.0	15.0	1.5	0.1	0.4
Lucerne	97.0	1.0	1.6	0.2	0.2
Uri	96.8	0.4	2.5	0.3	0.0
Schwyz	97.4	0.4	1.7	0.3	0.2
Obwalden	98.0	0.5	1.1	0.1	0.3
Nidwalden	97.6	0.6	1.5	0.2	0.1
Glarus	93.6	0.6	5.2	0.4	0.2
Zug	94.5	1.1	3.6	0.3	0.5
Fribourg	32.9	*65.7*	0.9	0.1	0.4
Solothurn	95.5	2.2	2.0	0.1	0.2
Basle Town	92.0	4.3	2.7	0.2	0.8
Basle Country	95.1	2.0	2.5	0.1	0.3
Schaffhausen	96.1	0.9	2.6	0.2	0.2
Appenzell- Outer Rhodes	97.5	0.4	1.5	0.2	0.4
Appenzell- Inner Rhodes	99.1	0.1	0.6	0.1	0.1
St. Gallen	96.9	0.5	2.0	0.4	0.2
Grisons	56.2	0.7	13.2	29.2	0.7
Aargau	96.8	1.0	1.8	0.2	0.2
Thurgau	96.4	0.5	2.7	0.2	0.2
Ticino	9.1	1.4	*88.8*	0.2	0.5
Vaud	11.1	*84.5*	2.9	0.1	1.4
Valais	33.2	*65.0*	1.6	0.0	0.2
Neuchâtel	11.8	*84.6*	3.1	0.1	0.4
Geneva	13.6	*77.6*	5.3	0.1	3.4

Annuaire statistique de la Suisse, 1953, p. 37.

All cantons had a German-speaking majority except for those whose percentages are in italic.

Italian that is spoken in everyday conversation is close to that spoken in France and Italy, the everyday language in German-speaking Switzerland is usually one of the many typically Swiss-German dialects.

The religious composition of Switzerland is no less complicated. The 1960 census reveals that 2,764,400 Swiss citizens, or 57.0 per cent are Protestants and that 2,038,200, or 42.1 per cent, profess Catholicism. The remaining 0.9 per cent is made up of other religions and those who profess no religion. The resident foreign population,

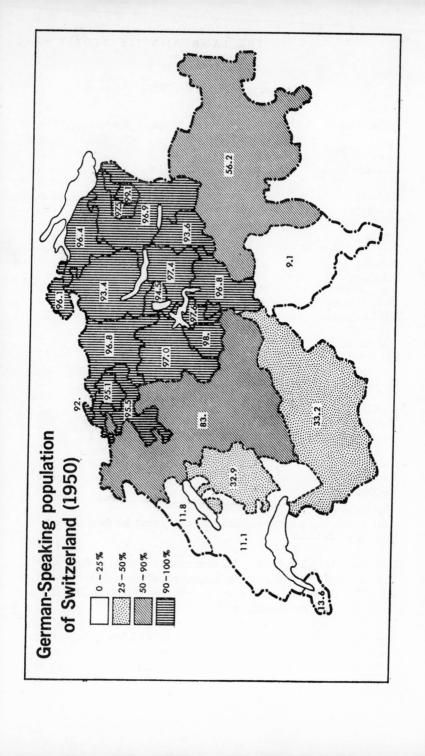

German-Speaking population
of Switzerland (1950)

0 – 25 %
25 – 50 %
50 – 90 %
90 – 100 %

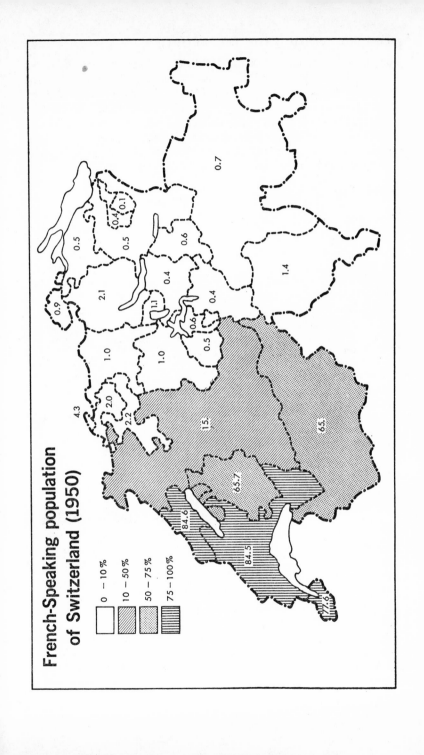

French-Speaking population of Switzerland (1950)

Legend:
- 0 – 10 %
- 10 – 50 %
- 50 – 75 %
- 75 – 100 %

on the other hand, is less equally divided. Catholics constitute the largest single group, 468,700, or 80.4 per cent, while Protestants provide only 93,200, or 16.0 per cent. The remainder is made up of those who profess another religion or those with no affiliation.

The cantons are almost evenly divided between those with a Catholic majority and those with a Protestant majority. In Table 4 these two groups of cantons are indicated together with the percentage enjoyed by the dominant religion according to the 1950 census.

Table 4

Dominant Religions in Swiss Cantons in 1950

Protestant Cantons — 11½	Protestant Population by percentage	Catholic Cantons — 10½	Catholic Population by percentage
Berne	83.8	Obwalden	96.1
Appenzell-Outer Rhodes	82.9	Valais	96.0
Vaud	78.1	Appenzell-Inner Rhodes	95.6
Neuchâtel	78.1	Schwyz	93.3
Schaffhausen	77.2	Uri	92.5
Basle Country	73.3	Nidwalden	92.0
Zurich	72.0	Ticino	91.7
Glarus	65.3	Fribourg	86.4
Thurgau	65.2	Lucerne	85.1
Basle Town	63.3	Zug	84.0
Aargau	56.9	St. Gallen	59.6
Grisons	50.7	Solothurn	55.5
Geneva	50.6		

Annuaire statistique de la Suisse, 1953, p. 40.

As the figures demonstrate, the religious breakdown does not necessarily follow the linguistic breakdown. Of the eleven and a half Protestant cantons, eight and a half are German-speaking, and three are French-speaking. The three French-Protestant cantons are Vaud, Neuchâtel, and Geneva. Of the ten and a half Catholic cantons, two are French-speaking, Fribourg and Valais, and one is Italian-speaking, Ticino. The remaining seven and a half cantons are both German-speaking and Catholic.

While the two major religions are fairly equally divided both on an overall basis and on a cantonal basis, the large cities are predominantly Protestant. In only one of the ten cities with a population larger than

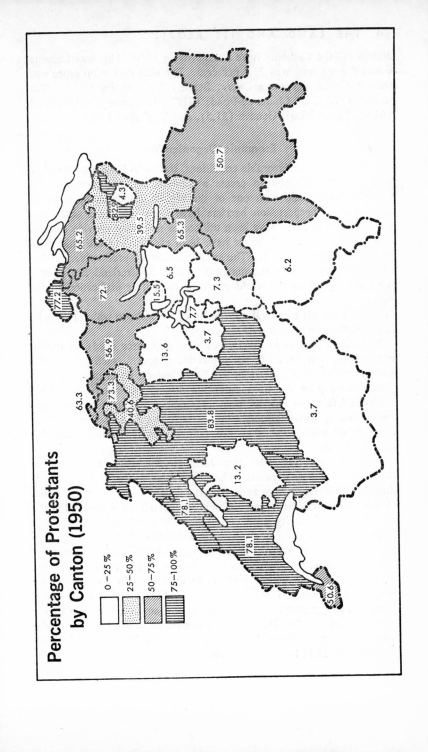

Percentage of Protestants
by Canton (1950)

0–25 %
25–50 %
50–75 %
75–100 %

30,000 did the Catholics have a majority in 1950. This was Lucerne, where the majority was 73.7 per cent. The nine Protestant cities with their Protestant percentages were: Berne (81.2), Bienne (79.2), Winterthur (77.1), La Chaux-de-Fonds (71.7), Lausanne (70.7), Zurich (64.9), Basle (62.6), Geneva (51.5), and St. Gallen (49.3).

Economic Organization

Despite less than favorable conditions, the Swiss have used imagination and determination to create a modern national economy that provides Switzerland with one of the highest standards of living in the world. Transportation barriers have been overcome. Electrical power and manpower have been utilized in tasks that provide a maximum return. Natural beauties have been exploited to the enjoyment of tourists from all lands. The small amount of productive soil has been made to produce the maximum yield. Switzerland has created for itself a place in the world economy far out of proportion to her size.

Table 5 affords a general impression of the tasks to which the Swiss have put their manpower over the years.

The steady decline in the Swiss agricultural force needs no special explanation. Despite all of the protective measures, such as subsidies and protective tariffs, taken by the Swiss Federal government to keep agriculture a profitable occupation, the normal movement toward the towns and factories has not been appreciably discouraged. Although the remaining Swiss farmers tend to make the best of the restricted acreages of arable soil, they are falling steadily behind increasing internal demand.

It is manufacturing rather than farming upon which the prosperity of Switzerland now depends. The labor force available to Swiss industry has increased from some 200,199 in 1895 to 750,453 in 1962. Of this total force, the largest single group (210,375) is engaged in the manufacture of quality products in the field of machinery, precision instruments, and diverse mechanical apparatus. Watchmaking, perhaps the oldest of Swiss industries, is still strong and by means of mechanization is tending to produce more goods with less personnel. In 1962 there were 66,043 workers in this area. In the metallurgic industry there were 97,277. The textile industry, which at one time employed 55 per cent of the labor force, now employs less than 10 per cent or a total of 70,440. Of the newer major industries, one of the most important is the manufacture of chemical products, which employed some 33,114 workers in 1962.

Table 5

Gainfully Employed by Types of Economic Activity

Year	Production from the Soil	Industry	Banking, Commerce, and Insurance	Hotels	Communications and Transportation	Civil Service and Professions	Household Servants and Day Laborers (Non-Agriculture)	Hospitals, Boarding Schools, Etc.[a]	Unemployed[b]
1888	37.7	41.4	4.6	2.5	2.7	3.9	7.2	*	*
1910	27.0	45.2	6.6	4.4	4.8	4.9	6.4	0.7	*
1920	26.1	43.5	7.9	4.0	4.9	5.4	6.3	1.9	*
1930	21.7	43.9	9.8	4.8	4.4	6.0	7.2	2.2	*
1941	21.2	43.2	10.0	4.3	3.8	7.4	6.0	2.7	1.4
1950	16.8	46.3	11.8	4.2	4.5	7.6	5.4	3.0	0.4

[a] A new category created in 1910. In French the word used is "établissements," and in German it is "Anstalten."

[b] Before 1941 the unemployed were tabulated with the economic group with which they were last affiliated.

The Swiss economy has always depended a great deal on international commerce. The early prosperity of many towns was a result of the movement of goods through the mountain passes. Later it was the export of mercenary soldiers that brought foreign gold into Swiss coffers. The nature of Switzerland's economic activity in the twentieth century, especially the manufacture of goods from imported raw materials, has made international commerce more important than ever to the prosperity of the country.

In 1962, for instance, goods exported by Switzerland were valued at some 9,579,940,000 Swiss francs. (A Swiss franc equals approximately 23 cents.) While the total value of Swiss exports falls behind that of many countries in western Europe, in percentage of the total national product, or in the per capita figures, it is one of the highest in the world. The most important single item of export in 1962 was machinery and spare parts, which attained the figure of 3,248,100,000 Swiss francs, followed by products of the chemical and pharmaceutical industry whose total value reached 1,798,000,000. The next important item was watches, which amounted to 1,428,900,000 Swiss francs. In 1962 the value of textile products was approximately 1,064,900,000 Swiss francs. The most important non-industrial item was cheese, whose value amounted to 158,000,000 Swiss francs.

Her close neighbors in Europe are still the best customers for Switzerland's products and sources of raw materials. Swiss prosperity no longer depends exclusively upon them, and the Swiss are constantly looking farther afield for markets. In 1934 the ten best customers of Switzerland were, respectively: Germany, France, Great Britain, Italy, the United States, the Netherlands, Belgium, Austria, Czechoslovakia, and Spain. In 1962 they were: Germany, United States, Italy, France, Great Britain, Netherlands, Austria, Belgium and Luxembourg, Sweden, and Spain. Tables 6 and 7 present the regional import and export picture for four representative years.

Table 6

Swiss Exports by Regions

(Percentages)

Year	Europe	Africa	Asia	North America	Latin America	Australia & Oceania
1900	79.1	1.0	4.4	12.2	2.8	0.5
1925	70.6	2.5	8.0	11.8	5.1	2.0
1950	61.7	3.9	7.6	15.8	10.0	1.0
1962	66.6	3.6	10.0	12.2	6.0	1.6

Table 7

Swiss Imports by Regions

(Percentages)

Year	Europe	Africa	Asia	North America	Latin America	Australia & Oceania
1900	86.4	1.8	2.8	5.7	2.7	0.6
1925	74.1	3.4	4.2	12.4	4.8	1.1
1950	58.0	6.4	6.9	17.7	10.1	0.9
1962	79.9	2.0	3.4	11.3	3.2	0.2

Switzerland has seldom been able to balance the cost of her imports with the value of her exports. In normal years the excess of the value of imports over exports runs from 10 per cent to 20 per cent. The deficit, however, is usually made up by the income from four other important money-making activities, tourism (the "industry of foreigners"), banking, insurance, and transport. Nothing need be said about the Swiss hotel industry except that much of it is concentrated in normally non-productive mountain areas and that it remains one of the best equipped and managed in the world. It has been estimated that in 1960, a good tourist year, tourism netted some 940,000,000 francs, the total deficit of imports over exports in the same year being 1,517,000,000 francs.

Deficit was turned into surplus in 1960 by the revenue from the three other important occupations of the Swiss, banking, insurance, and transport. The place of Switzerland in banking is well known throughout the world. Especially familiar is the tendency of money to fly into Swiss banks in times of world stress and crisis. Only recently, the Swiss announced that because of the large amount of flight capital coming into Swiss banks, certain types of accounts must now pay a handling charge rather than accrue interest. Estimates of "revenue from capital" in 1960 was some 680 million francs, augmented by about 125 million francs from the international insurance business. The transport of merchandise yielded 175 million francs.

The very basis of Swiss prosperity, however, makes it extremely vulnerable to conditions over which the Swiss have little or no control. Switzerland depends on other countries being in a position to purchase her goods and on the ability of foreigners to cross her borders and bring in the money to sustain the tourist industry. The earnings from flight capital deposited in her banks can never replace the income from exports and tourist trade. Consequently, any restrictions on free trade or the movement of tourists, including depressed economic conditions or an excess of protective tariffs, are the continuing concern of Switzerland. One of the more recent threats to the free movement of Swiss goods to important markets, the establishment of the European six-nation common market, and the manner in which Switzerland is attempting to meet that threat, will be discussed in a later chapter.

The prosperity of the Swiss economy has had two concomitant effects that are of special concern to the Swiss. One is the rise of Zurich as the most important industrial, commercial, and financial city in Switzerland. It is not the prosperity of Switzerland reflected in this development that causes concern, but the increasing concentration of power in one city and in one canton. Many Swiss, except perhaps the residents of Zurich itself, feel such growth poses a real threat to the decentralized cantonal structure of the Swiss federation and thus to one of the major sources of Swiss national strength.

The effect of prosperity on the Swiss citizen is also a source of anxiety. Some see abundance as a threat to the traditions of Switzerland and to the character of the individual Swiss. Evidences of this danger are found in the increasing desire for material goods and in the growing dependence of the Swiss economy on foreign labor to hold many of the less pleasant jobs, such as domestic service, hotel work, or unskilled labor in the fields and in industry. The question involved seems to be whether a luxury-seeking, materially oriented people can maintain their individuality and meet the challenges of the future. Switzerland, of course, is not alone in this dilemma.

✛ 2 ✛

Constitutional History

The history of Swiss political institutions is deceptively long. It is true that modern excavations have brought to light evidences of a Stone Age civilization on what is now Swiss territory, but the Swiss people did not live under anything approaching a unified government until late in the eighteenth century. On the other hand, if one should confine investigation of Switzerland only to that period following the eighteenth century, he would be guilty of overlooking information containing important clues to the explanation for many of the interesting and unique features of the present government.

Swiss constitutional history falls conveniently into four major periods: from the origins of Swiss history to the Treaty of Everlasting Alliance in 1291; from the Treaty of 1291 to the French Revolution; from the French Revolution to the Sonderbund War in 1847; and from the Constitution of 1848 to the modern period.

Origins

From a political point of view, there was little of significance in the history of Switzerland before the thirteenth century. Tribes had lived in the geographical area of present-day Switzerland far back in human history, witness the lake dwellers; but they were not known for much more than a propensity to engage in warfare. From another point of view, there was one important occurrence in this period that was to have a lasting effect on Swiss social and political evolution. That event was the invasion by the Germanic barbarians and the resulting establishment of the Swiss linguistic divisions. The western limit of that invasion turned out to be the Sarine River, running approximately down the middle of the canton of Fribourg, where it was halted by the

Burgundians, who had previously invaded from the west. In the south-east, only some of the higher Grison valleys escaped the Germanic invasion, and thus the inhabitants retained their Roman dialects. These linguistic divisions, imposed in the fifth and sixth centuries, have remained amost unchanged to modern times.

Because Switzerland came under the control of the Holy Roman Empire in the ninth and tenth centuries, it participated in the protracted fighting and suffering resulting from the imperial and the papal conflicts. From a Swiss point of view, the efforts of the German kings to secure the imperial crown did have a beneficial effect, however. As a consequence, traffic increased between Germany and Italy through the Swiss Alpine passes, and this commerce revived old cities and caused the creation of new communities.

The subsequent decline of the Empire's power in the thirteenth century thrust upon the commercial Swiss communities the necessity of providing more and more for their own defense and government. As the leading citizens organized the internal policing of their communities and the dispensing of justice, previously the Crown's most important activities, they became, in effect, free of imperial control. Experience in running their own affairs led the people of the communities to look askance at the subsequent attempts of the Hapsburgs to extend their authority over the Swiss valleys. In order to preserve their new-found independence, the Swiss turned first to the imperial government. Frederick II and his son, realizing that they had the power neither to defend the communities nor to force them to remain subservient, compromised by granting them charters as free communities within the Empire. The people of Uri received their charter in 1231 and those of Schwyz in 1240. If nothing else, the Emperor hoped to retain for himself free passage over the strategic Alpine passes.

When Rudolph of Hapsburg was elected king of Germany in 1273, both imperial and feudal overlordship over the two Swiss valleys passed into the same hands. Undoubtedly with an eye on the recently opened St. Gotthard route to Lombardy, Rudolph began to increase his holdings in central Switzerland and to exercise more actively his feudal rights over Uri and Schwyz. Although there was dissatisfaction, the Swiss did not let their discontent break out into the open during the lifetime of Rudolph.

The death of Rudolph on July 15, 1291, was the signal for action, however. To prevent further loss of liberty at the hands of Albert of Austria, Rudolph's heir, or perhaps to better participate in the general uprisings that were expected in the southwest portion of the empire, the leaders of Uri and Schwyz decided the time had come to seek strength in unity. Uri and Schwyz invited the authorities of Unter-walden, which had recently come under Hapsburg rule, to an urgent meeting to prepare a plan of action.[1]

The Old Confederation

From Three to Thirteen

The meeting of the leaders of the three small forest communities of Uri, Schwyz, and Unterwalden resulted in the creation of a "Perpetual League" for common defense, the actual beginning of Swiss political development. By the terms of the alliance, proclaimed in August, 1291, each community pledged to come to the aid of any member whose territory or rights were threatened. Furthermore, arbitration was to be used in settling all differences that should occur among them. Although they made no attempt to declare themselves free from the Empire, and in fact expressly recognized their feudal obligations, some limits were set on the types of bailiffs to be permitted in their respective territories. Despite the fact that the treaty of 1291 did not create a political entity, through its recognition of the principle of united strength it began the struggle to create for Switzerland an in-dependent place in the affairs of nations. August 1 is still observed as the Swiss national holiday.

For the next two hundred years, the constitutional history of Switz-erland is dominated not only by the increase in communities bound together by collective security pacts similar to that of 1291, but also by the success of these defense pacts. Lucerne joined the alliance in 1332; Zurich in 1351; Glarus and Zug in 1352; Berne in 1353; Fribourg and Solothurn in 1481; Basle and Schaffhausen in 1501; and Appenzell in 1513.

During this period the effectiveness of the Confederation was proved on many occasions. Despite forces superior in number and equipment, the original League decisively defeated Duke Leopold in 1315 when he tried to reimpose his family's authority on Schwyz and Unterwalden. As a confederation of eight, the Swiss defeated invading Austrian troops again at both Sempach in 1386 and Näfels in 1388. Duke Leopold of Austria was himself killed on the field of battle during the Sempach engagement. In 1475 Berne was caught raiding Burgundian territory in the Vaud at Louis XI's instigation. In accordance with their con-

---

[1] For a discussion of the reasons for this action, and the possibility that a mutual alliance of some sort had existed earlier, see E. Bonjour, H. S. Offler, and G. R. Potter, *A Short History of Switzerland* (London: Oxford University Press, 1952), pp. 70–85.

tractual obligations, the seven other members of the Confederation rushed to Berne's aid and defeated the Duke of Burgundy's counter-attacking troops at the battles of Grandson on March 22 and Morat on June 22, 1476.

As a league of ten cantons, the Swiss finally threw off the yoke of Empire. Maximilian was decisively defeated in the 1499 Swabian War after an attempt to lay claims on certain lands bordering on the confederation and to impose a new tax (Reichspfennig). By the terms of the peace of Basle, September 22, 1499, the Swiss were freed, in fact if not in name, from all imperial obligations.

The Confederation was also found to be an excellent offensive group, especially in times of unsettled national boundaries and conflicting territorial claims. For instance, lands were added to its holdings after Emperor Sigismund of Luxembourg expelled the Archduke of Austria from the Empire in 1415 and invited the Confederation to help itself to neighboring Austrian territory. Opportunities to acquire additional territory were especially good during the Italian wars of the sixteenth century. As a result of their reputation for fighting gained against the Austrians, Swiss soldiers were sought after by both sides. For their services Switzerland demanded important commercial and territorial concessions. Thus, in 1503, the three original cantons secured Bellinzona from Louis XII for the help of their troops in the Italian campaign. The Swiss troops turned against France in 1512, however, and occupied Locarno, Lugano, and southern Ticino. In 1513 they defeated the French forces sent to hold them in check and drove them out of Lombardy. After helping place Maximilian Sforza on the Milan throne, the Swiss marched into France to force Louis XII to recognize their Italian conquests. Even though the Swiss were able to force the French general defending Dijon to accept their terms, they were neither strong enough nor unified enough to impose them on the King.

In 1515 Francis I turned the tables on Switzerland by defeating its troops on the battlefield of Marignano. Needing Swiss soldiers for the reconquest of Milan, however, Francis I agreed to most of the terms previously demanded of Louis XII. The troops then fought on the French side and shared in the defeats at La Bicocca in 1522 and Pavia in 1525. Although for many years the Swiss continued to serve as mercenaries in various European armies, the defeats at French hands and as a French ally resulted in the cessation of most major warlike expeditions.

Despite the relative success of the Swiss troops on the field of battle, relations between the cantons were not always peaceful during the confederation's growth to thirteen. Sometimes there was strife between the smaller agrarian cantons and the strong commercial cities over economic policies or the division of spoils. At other times foreign policies of the various cantons caused unrest. For example, Zurich's long-standing policy of maintaining a close understanding with Austria, for reasons of commercial prosperity, irritated its neighbors. At one point in the fifteenth century, open war broke out between Zurich and Schwyz. Although ultimately they reunited to save Berne from defeat, other cantons were sharply critical of Berne's attempt to expand its influence in Burgundy. Relations among cantons were not helped when, during the Italian wars, Swiss mercenary troops were found on both sides of battle.

The Reformation and Its Legacy

The Reformation had both a short-term and a long-term effect on the development of Swiss political institutions. The most immediate effect was to further strain the already weak ties holding the thirteen cantons together. Four internal wars of religion were fought, in 1529, 1531, 1656, and 1712, mainly over the religion to be adopted in the Confederation's dependent territories. At one point there were actually two confederations existing side by side, one Protestant and one Catholic. Fortunately, however, a permanent split never developed. Although no mutual assistance pacts were renewed, none were renounced. In addition, the four religious wars were neither long nor bloody, nor was there any attempt on the part of the victors to subjugate their foes or crush them completely. In 1653 both Protestant and Catholic cantons were able to put aside their religious quarrels long enough to defeat an uprising of peasants that cut across cantonal boundaries.

The period of internecine strife was one of relative peace between Switzerland and its neighbors. The country remained neutral, for instance, in the Thirty Years War despite considerable pressure to gain its participation on either side, and by the Treaty of Westphalia, 1648, which brought the war to an end, Switzerland was finally made completely independent of the jurisdiction of the German Empire. With one exception, this was also a period without any significant gains in territory. The one major exception occurred in 1536 when Berne, notwithstanding the bitter opposition of the Catholic cantons, extended her control and the Protestant faith over all land in the present day canton of Vaud.

The long-term effect of the Reformation in Switzerland was the establishment of a permanent religious dualism. By the end of the second war the religious lines were fairly permanently drawn. While the majority of cantons in the Old Confederation chose to remain faithful to Catholicism, the more prosperous and populous cantons were converted to Protestantism. Thus Uri, Schwyz, Unterwalden, Lucerne, Zug, Fribourg, and Solothurn remained Catholic, while Zurich, Berne, Basle, and Schaffhausen became Protestant. In Glarus and Appenzell, where the two faiths were fairly evenly divided, each parish was left free to choose its preferred mode of worship. Appenzell later split into two independent parts along the lines of religious preference. Among the allies, the Republic of Geneva, the cities of Bienne, Mulhouse, and the town of St. Gallen became Protestant, whereas Valais and the Abbey of St. Gallen remained Catholic. The independent communities of the Grisons were divided, the majority choosing Protestantism. Almost all of the common holdings of the Confederation remained Catholic.

The Structure of the Old Confederation

In essence, the old Swiss Confederation was simply a series of alliances among thirteen small sovereign states, bound together by a common desire for security. The interlocking series of compacts and treaties that had been negotiated over the years pledged cantons both to come to one another's aid in the case of outside danger and to help suppress internal conflicts. Provision was made not only for arbitration of differences between cantons but also for administration, in some cases, of commonly held conquered territories.

The Diet, a periodic meeting of the sovereign representatives of the thirteen cantons, was the only body for the coordination of activities of the Confederation. Unanimity was the rule for each decision of importance, and each had to be ratified by all the member governments. The Old Confederation was even less of a political unit than the United States under the Articles of Confederation or the League of Nations. In effect, it was often difficult to tell whether there was a Swiss government at all.

The thirteen cantons in the Confederation possessed a wide variety of internal governments. Six of the older rural cantons were pure democracies in which the sovereign power was exercised by the *Landsgemeinde,* an annual assembly of all free citizens. These were Uri, Schwyz, Unterwalden, Zug, Glarus, and Appenzell. The cantons of Berne, Fribourg, Lucerne, and Solothurn were urban aristocracies in which the important families had adopted a system of representative democracy. Whereas sovereignty was legally vested in the whole body of free citizens, the real power was in the hands of a legislative body known as the Grand Council (Grand Conseil) of 100 to 200 members. Every male member of a ruling family could expect to sit in the Grand Council during his lifetime, and a few would be elected to the Executive Council (Petit Conseil) where the day-to-day administration of the canton was executed. Three cantons, Zurich, Basle, and Schaffhausen, were commercial oligarchies. Although their form of government was similar to that of the aristocracies, new recruits to the privileged families were more common.[2]

Despite equal representation in the meetings of the Diet, there existed among the thirteen cantons a definite hierarchy based on political, military, or economic importance. First in importance was Zurich, then Berne and Lucerne. In the second rank were grouped the five democracies of Uri, Schwyz, Unterwalden, Zug, and Glarus. In the bottom rank were Basle, Fribourg, Solothurn, Schaffhausen, and Appenzell. As regards the last one, Appenzell-Inner Rhodes had precedence over Appenzell-Outer Rhodes, as its representatives were quick to point out when it would be of advantage.

On the outskirts of the Old Confederation were numerous allies tied by treaties to one or more cantons. Among the allies were the Abbey of St. Gallen, the town of St. Gallen, the Leagues of the Grisons, the community of Valais, the town of Bienne, the town of Mulhouse, the ecclesiastical principality of Basle, the principality of Neuchâtel (whose nominal head was a Hohenzollern), and the Free Republic of Geneva.

All three types of cantons and most of their allies had subject territories over which they ruled as sovereign masters. In the cantons of Zurich, Berne, Lucerne, Basle, Fribourg, Solothurn, and Schaffhausen, the towns ruled over the countryside. In several rural cantons, one part was subject to another. There were also many areas which were subject to more than one canton. Some areas in western Switzerland, for instance, were ruled over by Berne and Fribourg while most of Ticino was the property of all cantons except Appenzell.

There were many weaknesses in the Old Confederation, therefore, on the eve of the French Revolution. First, no central government existed that could make binding decisions. The Diet could neither act quickly nor decide on such essential matters as military arrangements, citizenship, moneys, or tariffs. Cantons were sovereign in these areas, and the results were as varied as the cantons themselves. Second, there were many inequalities between cantons that caused friction. Rural cantons looked with suspicion at the wealth and influence of the urban cantons, and the small were jealous of the large. The aristocratic can-

[2] See Charles Gillard, *A History of Switzerland* (London: George Allen and Unwin, Ltd., 1955), pp. 47–50.

tons looked down on the commercial cantons, and the commercial cantons felt themselves superior to the rural. Third, there existed a serious element of inequality among individuals. Many individuals in the subject territories were little better than feudal serfs. Some in the richer cantons were able to make an adequate living, but not necessarily the living they wished, because many types of employment were exclusively in the hands of the privileged. Some who had political rights were not permitted to rise in politics beyond a certain level. Even in the *Landsgemeinde* cantons conditions were far from perfect. It has been estimated that some twenty thousand citizens who made up the electoral corps ruled over more than 300,000 without voting rights. As a result, Switzerland was just as susceptible as any other country to the appeals of eighteenth-century liberalism. After all, one of the greatest exponents of liberty, Voltaire, lived for a time in Geneva and the French border village of Ferney. Finally, there still remained the serious disruptive influences of opposing faiths which had not been extinguished by the Swiss religious wars.

The cohesive forces were few and only strong enough to keep the status quo under normal conditions. As stated by Rappard, the Old Confederation had behind it "the memories of battles waged in common and a like spirit of independence which revolted at all foreign oppression. . . ."[3] That and a common language were almost all that the Swiss had to counteract the forces, both philosophical and military, of the French Revolution. They proved to be inadequate.

In 1798 the armies of the French Revolution invaded Switzerland. Aided by local insurrectionaries who wanted a taste of the promised "liberty, equality, and fraternity," and by the Diet's inability to decide on the manner in which the country should be defended, the French forces broke the serious resistance offered by the Bernese and proceeded to occupy the Old Confederation.

The French Revolution and Its Consequences

The Constitution of 1798

Aided by a group of Swiss who honestly felt their country's need to be reorganized to meet the demands of changing times, the French bestowed a constitution on Switzerland which suddenly transformed it from a loose Confederation into a centralized and nominally democratic state. The new constitution was modeled after the French one,

[3] W. E. Rappard, *The Government of Switzerland* (New York: D. Van Nostrand Company, Inc., 1936), p. 16.

and its purpose was both to bring the benefits of French "civilization" to the people of Switzerland and to create a strong ally, or protectorate, at the crossroads of the Alps.

The new constitution proclaimed a centralized state, "one and indivisible." Cantons were transformed from independent units to administrative subdivisions of the central government along the lines of French "departments." The former subject territories and the allies of the Old Confederation were made new departments or parts of others. Thus Fribourg, Unterwalden, Uri, Zug, and Schwyz were enlarged, and eight new cantons were created: Léman, Argovie, Bellinzona, Lugano, Sargans, Thurgovie, Valais, and St. Gallen. The League of the Grisons, at the invitation of the French, became an integral part of the new state.

A bicameral national legislature was created consisting of a Senate and a Grand Council, each canton sending four representatives to the former and eight to the latter; and provision was made for the gradual replacing of cantonal laws by a single national law. Executive power, including the sole right to make treaties and to dispose of the armed forces, was deposited in a Directory of five members to be elected by the two legislative bodies. Each canton was permitted to retain a local legislature for restricted purposes, but, as on the French pattern, each had a prefect assigned to look after the interests of the national government.

The changes made in individual rights were no less revolutionary and in the long run had the more lasting impact. In addition to proclaiming a representative democracy as the only proper form of government, the 1798 Constitution completely eliminated the previous hierarchy among citizens. It created a single Swiss citizenship as well as common democratic suffrage. All hereditary rights of any character were abolished, and freedom of residence, trade, speech, and the press were guaranteed. Perhaps the ultimate demonstration of faith in the individual was contained in the provision subjecting the new constitution to a referendum.

Although there were a great many Swiss citizens who accepted the new constitution with enthusiasm, there remained a strong hard core who were not content to give up their hereditary rights and privileges. The ranks of the opposition grew as French interference in Swiss politics continued and as the Swiss were called upon to endure increasing sacrifices as a French ally. Open conflict soon broke out among the Swiss themselves, and between the Swiss and the French overlords, continuing in an increasing tempo throughout the five years the new constitution remained in force.

The Act of Mediation, 1803

In 1802, Napoleon, then First Consul of the French Republic, called the representatives of the various Swiss cantons to Paris to help draft a new constitution that would put an end to the internal Swiss conflicts. The result, called the Act of Mediation of 1803, turned out to be an excellent blend of ingredients tailored to meet local conditions and the needs, and brought ten years of peace as well. Even though much of the credit must be given to the Swiss representatives and their French counterparts, the final document was a reflection of the keen insight of the First Consul, who not only established the fundamental principles to be incorporated and supervised the work, but also approved the final draft.

In the first place, the Act of Mediation substituted federalism for the unworkable concept of a unitary state. In the center was placed a Diet, to which the six largest cantons sent two deputies each and the others one each. This body was given the power to establish a common currency, declare war and peace, raise an army and place it under a unified command, name ambassadors, and regulate the differences between cantons. Except for declarations of war and the conclusion of treaties of alliance, where a three-quarters majority was necessary, all other matters were to be decided by a simple majority vote.

Provisions were made for the Diet to meet alternately in the six major cantons, Fribourg, Zurich, Berne, Solothurn, Basle, and Lucerne. The canton in which the Diet was held was given the title Vorort, or leading canton, and the Burgomaster of the Vorort acted as the *Landammann,* or President, for that year. With these exceptions, Napoleon reinstated the old concept of equality among cantons. All powers not vested in the federal government were placed in the hands of the cantonal governments, and the cantons were permitted to retain the 1798 system of representative democracy or return to direct democracy, as some did. The thirteen original cantons were reconstituted, and six new cantons were created: St. Gallen, Grisons, Aargau, Thurgau, Ticino, and Vaud. It should be noted that the Act of Mediation, combined with the Constitution of 1798, made Switzerland a multi-lingual nation.

As regards individual rights, the Act of Mediation introduced another compromise. While retaining the principles of prohibiting special privileges, of complete freedom of movement, and of the right to choose an occupation, Napoleon did introduce a property qualification for voting.

This Act, although an excellent compromise between the needs for a strong state and the desire for local autonomy, did give rise to some discontent. The provisions permitting the French to use Swiss troops caused the most dissatisfaction. Although the original act called for 16,000 trained men, under Swiss pressure the levy was reduced to 12,000 in 1812.

Since the Act of Mediation was Napoleon's creation, it would have been expected to fall with him. The Swiss, however, lived up to their duties, at least symbolically, to the very end. On the morrow of the battle of Leipzig, the Allies called upon the Swiss to join the coalition to crush Napoleon. The Swiss refused to reply, declared the neutrality of Switzerland, and stationed some twelve thousand troops on the frontier. No resistance was made, nonetheless, when the 200,000 troops of the Allies were ordered to pass through Switzerland to attack the Emperor.

The Swiss Restoration

While the Act of Mediation can be described as an intelligent and moderate reaction to the Constitution of 1798, the new basic instrument, the Pact of 1815, drafted under pressure from the Allies, was impetuous and brutal. In one fell swoop, Switzerland turned its back on liberalism and progress and returned to the primitive tenets of the Old Confederation.

There were certain limits, however, beyond which the Allies would not allow the Swiss to go. Although the cantons were permitted to reinstate the forms of government existing under the Old Confederation, they were not permitted to recreate the old subject territories. The eight new cantons created by the Act of Mediation were permitted to remain; and three new ones that had been set free from French control, Valais, Neuchâtel, and Geneva, were admitted to the Confederation as equals. An article of the Pact of 1815 also decreed that political rights were not to be the privilege of any one class of citizens. The Swiss, however, interpreted that article narrowly, and before long cities in some cantons re-established their dominance over the rural areas, aristocracies controlled political matters, and old guilds regained their economic advantages.

At the center of the Confederation was placed a modified version of the old Diet. Although each canton was given one vote as before, the old rule of unanimity on important questions gave way to a three-quarters majority. Berne, Zurich, and Lucerne were named the leading cantons, Vororts, and the principal officials of each were given a chance to direct federal affairs for a period of two years. The only permanent organ that remained under the Pact of 1815 was the Federal Chancellery, or secretariat, which traveled from canton to canton with the Vorort. While the cantons resumed most of the functions of sovereign states, the Diet was given not only control of contingents of soldiers from each member canton, along with an annual monetary contribution for a central war fund, but also power to use the troop contributions to provide for defense and maintain internal order. As a final capstone to their handiwork, the Allies at the Congress of Vienna recognized, and guaranteed as some say, perpetual neutrality on the Swiss Confederation.

For fifteen years there was peace and prosperity, and the newly emerged aristocratic rulers were content to relax somewhat their old tyrannical rule in return for the restoration of old privileges. Both internal and external events were in preparation, however, that were to lead to another significant change in the Swiss system of government.

The first event was the July, 1830, revolution in France which brought into the open Swiss liberal sentiments not extinguished by the Pact of 1815. Among the reforms demanded were direct election of legislators, open legislative sessions, liberty of the press, right of petition, and legal guarantees of personal and property rights. In quick succession most of these demands were presented and accepted by the legislatures of nine cantons without recourse to bloodshed. The cantons thus affected were Ticino, Thurgau, Zurich, Aargau, Solothurn, Lucerne, St. Gallen, Fribourg, and Schaffhausen. Although some violence occurred in Berne, it likewise quickly gave way to the reform movement. In the canton of Basle, a clash between the liberal forces in the countryside and the conservative town led to a civil war which ended in 1833 with the separation of Basle into the two half-cantons of Basle Town and Basle Country. As would be expected, these cantons brought pressure to bear for a revision of the 1815 Pact along more liberal lines. In the face of strong resistance from the conservative cantons, they were at first unsuccessful.

Events came to a head, however, when the liberal movement collided with Catholic conservatism over such questions as the taxation of church property, abolition of monasteries, and exclusion of the Jesuits. In Aargau, Geneva, Valais, and Zurich political passions resulted in armed conflict and bloodshed. In order to defend themselves against the pressure of the liberal cantons and to put down internal liberal movements, the Catholic cantons of Lucerne, Uri, Schwyz, Unterwalden, Zug, Fribourg, and Valais formed a separate league within the Confederation, the Sonderbund. An appeal for outside help was also under consideration by the Sonderbund when the Diet demanded that the Sonderbund dissolve itself. After receiving a blunt refusal, the Diet sent an army of 100,000 into the field to dissolve the league by force. Under General Dufour as Commander in Chief, the federal troops completely crushed the rebellion in a short nineteen-day campaign, November 10 to November 29, 1847. As a result of British intervention and European revolutions which broke out at about the same time, Austria, France, and Prussia were prevented from interfering until too late.

There were, in the first half of the nineteenth century, several forces that led the victorious liberal cantons to the conclusion that the Pact of 1815 could no longer meet the needs of Switzerland. The first and most important of these was undoubtedly the need for security, both internal and external. The Pact had shown its weakness on several occasions as regards internal security, and few doubted that it would be any more effective in the face of strong external forces. Many people had disliked the constant interference of the Allies in Swiss internal affairs, but realized that the strength to resist it did not exist. The second factor was economic. The growth of the Swiss economy had been hampered by internal conflict. There was also a sad lack of uniformity in such essential matters as money, weights and measures, and postal communication, to say nothing of the lack of consistency in customs duties both between cantons, and between cantons and foreign states. These obstacles were particularly severe in a country limited in natural resources. The third factor was political. Many Swiss who were not in the privileged classes remembered the taste of liberty and equality offered to them by the Constitution of 1798. These forces of liberalism had been reinforced by the growth of a new middle class which had gained economic power but which had been refused political power by the privileged classes.

Modern Switzerland

With the conservative cantons in no position to complain, the victors of the Sonderbund War drafted a new liberal constitution the provisions of which, with only minor revisions, remain the fundamental law of Switzerland to this day. The government they created was basically similar to that of the Act of Mediation, with American overtones, and the individual rights it guaranteed were those of the 1798 Constitution. This section will present an overall review of the historical evolution of the Constitutions of 1848 and 1874. Details will be dealt with in the following chapters.

Drafting the Constitution of 1848

The Constitution of 1848 was essentially the creation of a committee of twenty-three men elected by their colleagues in the Diet or, in the case of a few recalcitrant cantons, appointed by its Chairman. As members of the Diet, most were also chiefs of their cantonal governments. The ones who came from the liberal cantons had also participated in the liberal revision of their cantonal constitutions. The large majority were members of the legal profession, supplemented by a few merchants, two doctors, and a few high-ranking officers who had just returned from the Sonderbund War. Perhaps the most interesting characteristic of the participants was their relative youth. Four, including the chairman of the committee, were in their thirties, the great majority were in their forties, and only six were over fifty. The senior member of the committee was fifty-eight years of age.[4] Only Neuchâtel, which was still nominally a principality under the King of Prussia, and Appenzell-Inner Rhodes were not represented on the drafting committee.

After thirty-one sessions, held in secret so that the members could work without outside pressures, the committee presented the Diet with a completely new constitution, 104 articles in length. To gain time, the draft along with the report of its chairman were submitted directly to the cantonal governments so that their representatives could be instructed.

From May 15 to June 27, 1848, the Diet examined the draft in detail, along with the comments of the cantonal governments. After only minor changes, and despite the fervent opposition of the small Catholic cantons, the draft was approved by the Diet and submitted to all the cantons with the request that they make their approval or disapproval known no later than September 1, 1848.

On September 12, 1848, the Diet announced that the new constitution had been approved by fifteen and a half cantons, representing a population of 1,898,887 and had been rejected by six and a half cantons with a population of 292,371. The six and a half cantons which opposed the adoption of the new constitution included five of the cantons of the old Sonderbund: Uri, Schwyz, Unterwalden, Valais, Zug, and Appenzell-Inner Rhodes. Over the objection of the three forest cantons, the originators of the Swiss confederation, the Diet announced the adoption of the new constitution for all of Switzerland.

[4] W. E. Rappard, *La Constitution fédérale de la Suisse* (Neuchâtel: Éditions de la Baconnière, 1948), p. 111.

Some Compromises

In order to achieve a strong, stable federal state, the drafters of the 1848 Constitution adopted several compromises that make the Swiss Federal Government basically different from other European governmental systems. The first compromise was that of adopting a bicameral legislature. In the beginning both of the major factions wanted a unicameral system. One group advocated a single legislative house in which cantons would be represented on the basis of population. It was felt that this system would better reflect the increased duties and sacrifices demanded of larger cantons in a unified state, as well as be more compatible with the liberal tradition of representation based on population. The supporters of local autonomy, "federalists" in Swiss usage, were afraid of the centralizing tendency that would result from a single popularly elected body and, of course, knew that they would be outvoted by the larger cantons. They preferred a single legislative body in which each canton had equal representation. While both factions thus preferred a single legislative body, neither group was strong enough to force its point of view. Despite expressions on both sides of abhorrence for "foreign institutions," a bicameral system based on the American model became the only acceptable compromise.

The Swiss did not adopt the American type of executive, however. The idea was discussed but found to be repugnant to the liberal philosophy of placing all power in the hands of the peoples' representatives. Swiss memories of experiences at the hands of tyrannical usurpers of power were also significant in the decision to reject such an office. On the other hand, an executive of some type was considered essential to the smooth working of the new federal state. The drafters of the 1848 Constitution finally decided to borrow from cantonal experience and create a collegiate executive of seven men.

The liberal philosophy also militated against giving a court the right to declare acts of a duly elected legislature invalid. Thus, although a high court was created, it was not given the power of judicial review. As a concession to the "federalists" only one federal court was established and not an entire system. Cantonal courts were given jurisdiction over federal matters.

While other details of the 1848 Constitution and their application will be dealt with in other sections of this work, one immediate result of the increased stature of the new Swiss state should be mentioned at this point. Although the canton of Neuchâtel had been given equal footing with other Swiss cantons after 1814, it had also been under the nominal control of the kings of Prussia. While the King of Prussia had frowned upon a revolt in Neuchâtel in 1848 that had brought the liberals to power, other affairs had prevented him from doing anything about the matter. The subduing of a counterrevolution by federal forces in 1856, however, brought about a round of serious discussions between Prussia and Switzerland. With the help of France and England, but mostly as a consequence of the strengthened Swiss position resulting from the 1848 Constitution and a determination to go to war if necessary, Frederick William IV finally relinquished all his claims on Neuchâtel.

The Constitution of 1874

While the Swiss have had frequent recourse to the amending procedure, as will be documented later, there has been only one general revision. For the most part, this revision, which took place in 1874, supplemented rather than changed the work that had been done in 1848. It strengthened the federal government in military matters in order to overcome the weaknesses observed in the army during mobilization in 1870–71; it reinforced the anti-clerical provisions of the 1848 Constitution; and it added new federal powers to combat some of the abuses that had been observed in the economic system.[5]

Although innovations in structure were few, the revision of 1874 did introduce the federal legislative referendum. The constitutional initiative was not introduced until 1891, nor the optional referendum on treaties until 1921.

[5] For a detailed account of the period 1848 to 1874, see Bonjour and others, pp. 302–342.

✛ 3 ✛

Federalism and Civil Rights

The framers of the Swiss Constitution of 1848 had before them the normal task of most modern constitution makers: to create a system of government that would provide security against external enemies and internal conflicts and furnish the conditions necessary for the attainment of a good life for a maximum number of individuals. They also had before them a series of obstacles to overcome, many of which were peculiar to Switzerland: severe religious differences, linguistic pluralism, limited natural resources, and past reliance upon the canton as the principal unit of government. In the solution that was chosen, three principles stand out: federalism, liberalism, and democracy.

The emphasis on federalism was considered necessary not only to create unity but also to recognize the historical importance of the cantonal units and the cultural differences that existed among them. The emphasis on liberalism, and the individual rights that that term implied, took into account the influences, direct and indirect, of the French Revolution. Nothing but continual strife could be expected if Swiss citizens were not given written guarantees that they would be free from all past forms of personal subjugation whether from a titled aristocracy, a commercial aristocracy, or a church. Finally, as a part of the liberal trend, and also as a recognition of the need to create a new sense of individual responsibility for the future of the new Swiss state, the founders emphasized the direct participation of the Swiss citizen in the functioning of government.

The great length of the Swiss Constitution in comparison to that of the United States, for example, is due largely to the detail with which the drafters spelled out their version of these concepts. Although modified by the major revision of the Constitution in 1874, partial revisions that followed, and day-to-day practice of government, these concepts remain essentially valid to this day. Before proceeding, it should be noted that since the Swiss Constitution goes into considerably more detail than does its American equivalent, there is far less reliance in Switzerland upon "implied powers" than there is in the United States.

This chapter will be devoted primarily to an examination of the Swiss versions of federalism and civil rights and their development over the years. The Swiss version of democracy will be treated in the following chapter.

Federalism

In the first place it must be recognized that despite the wording used in Article 1 of the Swiss Constitution, "the twenty-two sovereign cantons," and despite the tenacity with which the people defend the "sovereignty" of their cantons, the Swiss national governmental system fits easily into a definition of a federation. There is a division of powers between the central and the local governments which has been made by a superior authority, the Constitution, and which cannot be changed by either acting independently.

Before going on to investigate the proportion of sovereignty awarded to each of the governmental units, and to ascertain whether or not the general tendency for the central unit to increase its power over local units is true in Swiss experience as it is elsewhere, a word or two devoted to the composition and characteristics of the Swiss cantons is indicated.

The Cantons

The official order of precedence of the twenty-two Swiss cantons is prescribed in Article 1 of the Swiss Federal Constitution. This order, including the dates of entry into the Swiss system, is as follows: Zurich (1351), Berne (1353), Lucerne (1332), Uri (1291), Schwyz (1291), Unterwalden (Obwalden and Nidwalden) (1291), Glarus (1352), Zug (1352), Fribourg (1481), Solothurn (1481), Basle (Town and Country) (1501), Schaffhausen (1501), Appenzell (the two Rhodes) (1513), St. Gallen (1803), Grisons (1803), Aargau (1803), Thurgau (1803), Ticino (1803), Vaud (1803), Valais (1815), Neuchâtel (1851), and Geneva (1815). As is apparent, with the exception of the first three, the order of precedence of the twenty-two cantons is based on seniority. In recognition of their special positions of importance and influence in the old confederal system, Zurich, Berne, and Lucerne were given precedence over all other cantons. If the first three listings were to be based on present-day influence, Lucerne would undoubtedly be replaced by one of the larger cantons such as Vaud.

Unterwalden, Basle and Appenzell are each divided into half-cantons: Obwalden and Nidwalden, Basle Town and Basle Country, and Appenzell-Inner Rhodes and Appenzell-Outer Rhodes. Since each of the half-cantons has its own autonomous government, the number of subordinate units in the Swiss federation is actually twenty-five. In general, however, the half-cantons are only half as "sovereign" as their full-fledged sisters. Whereas half-cantons have only one vote in the Council of States, full cantons have two. In addition, the former count for only a half in constitutional referendums. In only a few unimportant areas, such as the seldom used procedure for originating legislation, are the powers of the cantons equal.

The cantonal separations occurred at three major junctions of Swiss history and for three entirely different reasons. Unterwalden split in the fifteenth century, during the beginning of the Old Confederation, because of the difficulty of communication between its two major valleys. Appenzell broke into two parts in 1597 as a result of the Reformation when Outer Rhodes turned to Protestantism while Inner Rhodes clung to Catholicism. The final split, between Basle Town and Basle Country, occurred in 1833 during the Swiss liberal reform movement and was precipitated by a refusal of the rural population to remain subject to the control of its urban brethren. Since the three cantons were quite small at the time of the rupture, there was little desire to give them a status equal to the others. Thus, to recognize their inferior status, and simultaneously to preserve theoretical equality of all the units, half-cantons were created.

The Swiss have been reasonably content with their nineteen full cantons and six half-cantons. Only two suggested changes have caused more than local interest, the proposal to reunite the two Basles and the contrasting proposal to divide the canton of Berne. The first movement has been fomented by the steady encroachment of urban Basle upon the formerly agricultural areas of Basle Country. In reality, at the present time Basle Town and Basle Country are no more than a large city and its suburbs. The consequent difficulties of coordination of policies, duplication of services, and problems of taxation are all stressed by the proponents of unification.

On two occasions the matter has been brought to the attention of the federal government. In 1947, after obtaining the support of a majority of the voters of the two half-cantons, the governments of Basle Town and Basle Country presented the National Assembly with a request for unification couched in terms that the two half-cantons wished the federal government to approve a new single constitution. It was pointed out that at the time of the original division it had been agreed that they could reunite at any future date that it was found to be desirable. The Council of States refused to give the requested approval in December, 1947, and the National Council refused in March, 1948. The main reason given was that a constitutional amendment was necessary for approval, rather than an action by the legislature, since the names of both half-cantons appear in Article 1 of the Constitution and since Article 5 obliges the federal government to assure the territorial integrity of each canton. Although Article 5 refers only to "cantons," it was considered that it also meant "half-cantons."[1]

In 1960, the partisans of unity in Basle Country initiated a new demand for union that was approved by a vote of 16,500 to 12,000. After this success in the area where most of the opposition had been forthcoming, the Grand Councils of the two half-cantons petitioned the federal legislature to reconsider its decisions of 1947 and 1958. This request was successful. In March and June, 1960, the National Assembly approved new provisions in the constitutions of Basle Town and Basle Country which set forth the procedures for reunification. The Council of States approved by a vote of twenty-five to one, and the National Council by 111 to 15.[2] A constitutional commission, made up of representatives of the two cantons, met for the first time on November 28, 1960, to begin the task of drafting a new unified constitution. The draft will first be presented to the electors of the two cantons for their approval, then to the Federal Assembly for its approval, and finally the people and the cantons of Switzerland will be asked to accept the necessary modification to Article 1 of the Constitution. Although this work will probably take a number of years to complete, the decisions of the Federal Assembly in March and June, 1960, practically insure that Basle will once again become a single canton.

It is a little difficult for an outsider to understand why such a simple change, desired by a majority of both of the half-cantons, should take so long and lead to so much discussion. There are two major elements that may account for it. The first is the traditional Swiss conservatism that looks askance at any attempt to change the status quo. After all, Switzerland has gotten along with six half-cantons for over a hundred years. The second element is undoubtedly the dislike of creating a precedent of changing the structure of the Confederation without re-

[1] See below, pp. 40–41.
[2] *Feuille fédérale*, 1960, II, p. 221.

sorting to a constitutional amendment and the resulting approval of the people, an old agreement notwithstanding. To better understand this fear of creating a precedent, one should consider it in conjunction with the second suggested change, the division of Berne.

The Berne situation, in contrast to that of Basle, is one of controversy. It is not a matter of how best to achieve an agreed end but a clash between two opposing points of view. Basically, some of the French-speaking citizens of the Bernese Jura wish to be separated from the German-speaking Bernese of the rest of the canton. Berne had been a German-speaking canton exclusively until 1815 when it was given the French-speaking Jura (the old Bishopric of Basle) as a compensation for giving up Vaud and some other subject territories. The complaints of the Jurassians are many, including the general one used by almost all aspirants to independence — that the majority neglects the best interests of the minority. Among the specific complaints are that not enough cantonal taxes find their way back to the Jura, that the minority is not given its rightful place in the cantonal government, and that the Jurassians do not have an adequate voice in decisions concerning the watchmaking industry, of which the Bernese Jura provide the greater part of the total Swiss output.

There does not seem to be, as in the case of Basle Town and Country, the possibility of an early or easy solution to the Bernese affair. A cantonal initiative for the division of Berne in July, 1959, was narrowly rejected by the Jurassian voters and failed by a wide margin in the canton as a whole. This upset has not deterred the secessionists, however, as they feel that the majority sentiment in the area affected should be the deciding factor and are anxious to bring the problem to the federal government for a nation-wide decision. In the national area, it is hoped that the separatists will receive help from the French-speaking cantons and others who might be willing to embarass the Bernese majority. The majority, on the other hand, argues that it is a domestic affair. It must be admitted that most Swiss consider the separatist movement the hobby of a small active minority without real support or serious cause, and without any chance of a successful outcome. Nevertheless, the Bernese affair is disturbing to many, and the separatists are likely to keep the issue alive for many years to come.[3]

[3] An example of the type of thing that can be expected was the attempt of the separatists in April, 1960, to defeat a candidate for the Bernese legislature on the basis that he had made slighting remarks about the Jura. The individual in question, Mr. Hans Tschumi of Interlaken, had opposed giving a citizen of Jura the administrative direction of cantonal public works in a speech before the Bernese Grand Council in 1947 on the grounds that a department of such general importance should have at its head a man whose mother tongue was German. See *Journal de Genève* (April 22, 1960), 2.

Guarantees and Obligations

"The Confederation guarantees to the cantons their territory, their sovereignty . . . , their constitutions, the liberty and rights of their people and the constitutional rights of citizens, and the rights and powers conferred by the people on the authorities."[4] Article 16 of the Constitution authorizes the Federal executive to take any necessary measures, within the limits of its power, to enforce these guarantees. This would include, in cases of extreme urgency, the raising and using of up to 2,000 troops. If more are needed, or if they remain on duty for more than three weeks, the agreement of the Federal legislature must be obtained. (This limitation on the use of troops is general and not confined to federal intervention to enforce the constitutional guarantees.) Every canton is obliged to allow the free passage of troops across its territory. Further, if a canton is not in a position to call for aid, the Swiss federal government may intervene on its own initiative.

According to Professor Sauser-Hall, nine actions on the part of the federal government in cantonal affairs between 1848 and 1956 can be classified as "intervention" within the meaning of Article 16: (1) Ticino in 1855, 1889, and 1890; (2) Geneva in 1864, 1902, and 1932; (3) Neuchâtel in 1856; (4) Zurich in 1871; and (5) Basle and Zurich in 1919.[5] A wide variety of situations triggered these interventions. The Ticino intervention of 1890, for instance, came after a particularly bloody uprising in which the revolutionists had actually overthrown the cantonal government. The intervention in Zurich in 1871 was engendered by a fight between interned French soldiers and celebrating Germans that was beyond the power of the Zurich authorities to control. At Geneva in 1902, riots resulting from a general strike were controlled by the Genevese officials before the authorized 2,000 federal troops were brought into action. In several cases the federal authorities did not wait until internal order was actually disturbed nor did they await a call for help from the cantonal authorities. Both the Ticino case of 1889 and the Geneva case of 1864, for instance, were undertaken on the strength of private communications predicting disorder. In the earlier interventions, the federal powers appointed a "commissioner" who took over the military operations and assumed such powers in the civil field in the name of the Confederation as he considered necessary. In the Geneva intervention of 1932 a "commissioner" was not used.

[4] Art. 5.
[5] Georges Sauser-Hall, *Guide Politique Suisse* (Lausanne: Payot, 1956), p. 99.

Although the number of federal interventions in cantonal affairs may seem excessive, the statement of Professor Brooks is still valid: "It must be remembered, however, that prior to the establishment of the present republic the pages of Swiss history were marred by constantly recurring outbreaks of serious disorders and insurrection. Instead of evidences of instability, therefore, the relatively few and mild disturbances that have occurred since 1848 are really indices of the strength and decision of federal power."[6] Professor Brooks' statement gains additional strength when it is noted that no such federal intervention in the affairs of cantons has occurred since 1932. Certain other countries have not been as stable.

Further, cantons must submit all new constitutions, or modifications to existing constitutions, to the federal goverment for its approval ("guarantee" in the Swiss usage). Approval is usually given in the form of a federal *arrêté*. If approval is denied, the cantons must remove the unacceptable passage or passages. Acts committed under the provisions of an approved constitution can, of course, still be challenged for conformity to federal law.

In general, a cantonal constitution or a revision thereof will be accepted only if (1) it contains "nothing contrary to the provisions of the federal Constitution"; (2) it assures "the exercise of political rights according to republican forms — representative or democratic"; and (3) it has been "accepted by the people and can be amended when an absolute majority of citizens so demand."[7] By enumerating the two forms of "republican" government, the Swiss effectively prevented any disputes over the compatibility of direct democracy with a republican form of government, as occurred in the United States.[8]

There are several other obligations that the Constitution imposes on the cantons in the interest of eliminating threats to the federal system. Many of these rules are not too important in present-day use, having been introduced in 1848 to counteract what the framers of the Constitution felt to be more or less immediate dangers. Thus, Article 7 forbids "all separate alliances and treaties of a political character between cantons." The Sonderbund War which immediately preceded the writing of the 1848 Constitution had stemmed directly from a political alliance between a group of Catholic cantons. On the other hand, the same article permits "conventions" among cantons "on matters of legislation, administration, or justice." In a federation where the lower

---

[6] Robert C. Brooks, *Government and Politics of Switzerland* (New York: World Book Company, 1921), pp. 57–58.

[7] Art. 6.

[8] *Pacific Sales Telephone and Telegraph Co.* v. *Oregon*, 223 U.S. 118 (1912).

units retain independent power, such agreements are often necessary for the proper running of day-to-day affairs. Agreements between two cantons to control the exploitation of water power, for example, or multilateral agreements among several cantons to lay down rules for the support of the poor and invalid are not uncommon in Switzerland.

Agreements between a canton and a foreign power are restricted to such matters as public economy and police regulations. Such compacts, along with conventions between cantons on legislative, administrative and judicial matters, must be brought to the attention of the federal authorities who may prevent their execution if they are found to "contain anything prejudicial to the Confederation or to the rights of other Cantons."9 The number of treaties between cantons and foreign countries is not large, and the modern trend is to leave such matters to the federal government. As concerns the few that remain: "It seems that the party bound by them in international law is the Confederation and not the Canton."10

Just as the Confederation is not authorized to maintain a standing army, the troops that the cantons can maintain are limited. According to Article 13 of the Swiss Constitution: "No canton or half-canton may, without the permission of the federal government, maintain a standing force of more than 300 troops." The 300 men does not include the cantonal police. In addition, neither the cantons nor the federal government may negotiate "capitulations" with a foreign power by which the recruitment of mercenaries is permitted on Swiss soil in exchange for money or other forms of payment. Before 1848 the negotiations of capitulations were regular occurrences. Not only does this provision make formal agreements between governmental units illegal, with the exception of providing Swiss Guards for the Vatican (which is not considered as "military duty"), but the service of individuals in foreign armies has been made an offense under Swiss military law. In a further effort to make Switzerland the sole object of Swiss loyalty, Article 12 provides that: "Members of the federal authorities, civil and military officials, and federal representatives or commissioners, members of cantonal governments and legislative assemblies, may not accept from a foreign government any pension, salary, title, gift, or decoration." An infringement of this rule involves loss of office or function. Further, no officer, noncommissioned officer, or private soldier may accept an order or title conferred by a foreign government.

9 Art. 9, para. 2.
10 Christopher Hughes, *The Federal Constitution of Switzerland* (Oxford: Clarendon Press, 1954), p. 12.

The Constitution also imposes certain obligations on cantons in their interrelationships, some superfluous in the light of present-day federal authority, being aimed at the evils of a loose confederation, and others important to the smooth working of inter-cantonal affairs. In the former category is the provision that: "When a dispute arises between two cantons they shall not take any action nor resort to arms," but are to submit the dispute to the decision of the Federation.[11] Also in the same category is the provision that, in the case of threat from a foreign country, a canton "must invoke the assistance of the confederated states," and: "The cantons so called upon are bound to give their assistance."[12] Of more practical importance are Articles 60 and 61 which perform a function similar to that of Article IV, Sections 1 and 2 (clause 1) of the American Constitution. Article 60 provides that: "Every canton is bound to accord to citizens of other confederate states the same treatment that it accords its own citizens as regards legislation and judicial proceedings." Article 61 reads: "Final judgments in civil cases delivered in one canton are enforceable throughout Switzerland."

Division of Powers

In the first place, the Swiss Constitution establishes the general principle that the federal government exercises delegated powers while the cantons retain all residual powers. Article 3, which is similar to the corresponding provision in the United States Constitution, reads: "The cantons are sovereign so far as their sovereignty is not limited by the federal Constitution, and, as such, they exercise all the rights which are not delegated to the federal power."

In quantity and scope, however, the powers granted to the Swiss federal government by the Constitution are much broader than is the case in the United States. Among the powers that are similar, are those giving the Swiss federal government control over foreign affairs, the army (with certain exceptions), customs and duties (both export and import), the coinage of money, issuing of banknotes, weights and measures, extradition, and the movement of foreigners. A further group of delegated powers carries the scope of the Swiss federal government's powers beyond that of the United States, but not necessarily that of other governments with a federal system. These include the granting of a federal monopoly over the manufacture and sale of gunpowder, telegraphs and telephones, broadcasting and television, and alcohol.

[11] Art. 14.
[12] Art. 15

The Swiss federal government also has been given wide powers in the area of commerce and, contrary to the situation in the United States, there is no artificial division between interstate and intrastate commerce. The federal powers include general legislative authority over ship and aerial navigation, automobiles, food and drugs, and supervision over such roads and bridges "in the maintenance of which it is concerned."[13] The Swiss federal government runs all the major railways in the country. It has legislative control over what would appear to an American to be local issues, hunting and fishing, water and forests, water power, and infectious diseases. The federal government, rather than the cantons, has been empowered to legislate on matters of civil, criminal, and commercial law, including such specific matters as right of marriage and the collection of debts. As if the federal government did not have enough with which to occupy itself, it has recently been given a wide constitutional grant of power in the field of social legislation including the right to legislate for the elimination of unemployment, to protect the family, and to provide for a minimum of social security.

It must also be noted that Article 2 of the Transitory Provisions of the Swiss Federal Constitution has been interpreted to mean that "federal law breaks cantonal law." Thus in any case where the two come into conflict, the cantonal law is considered to be void. Further, the Swiss do not have a supreme court in the American sense that there is a body with the power of judicial review.

The question immediately arises as to the areas in which the canton remains sovereign. The answer seems to be that there are no areas of government in which the cantons retain a completely free hand: the Constitution gives the Swiss federal government at least a supervisory function in all aspects of political life. This does not mean, however, that Switzerland has a unitary form of government. Federalism is kept alive, and flourishing in Switzerland by means of two main expedients, by giving the cantons "primary" responsibility in certain areas and by relying heavily on the cantonal governments for the execution of federal laws.

In the former category are the functions normally left to the local units in federal systems, such as maintenance of law and order, health and sanitation, public works, and education. The latter is an excellent example. Article 27 of the Swiss Federal Constitution reads as follows:

> The Confederation has the right to establish, in addition to the existing federal polytechnic school, a federal university and other

[13] Art. 37.

institutions of higher education or to subsidize institutions of this nature.

The Cantons shall provide for primary education, which must be adequate and exclusively under the control of the civic authorities. It is compulsory and, in the public schools, free.

The public schools shall be such that they can be attended by members of all religious faiths without offence to their freedom of conscience or belief.

The Confederation will take the necessary measures against cantons which fail to fulfill these obligations.

Thus, in elementary education the cantons are given primary responsibility. However, the standards that the cantons must maintain — adequate, obligatory, non-sectarian, and free — are laid down by the Constitution, and the federal government is given the power to enforce them. Although one attempt on the part of the federal government to establish a body to keep the cantonal primary schools under close supervision was rejected in a referendum as an attempt to centralize the control of all primary education, in 1902 a large majority of the popular vote and all except one canton approved the following addition to Article 27:

Article 27 *bis.* Subsidies shall be granted to the cantons to help them fulfil their obligations in respect to primary education.

. . . .

The organization, direction and supervision of elementary schools remain within the authority of the cantons, subject to Article 27 of the Federal Constitution.[14]

In university education, the federal government has taken another tack. While it maintains the technical university mentioned in Article 27, it has refused to create a federal university and other institutions of higher learning. Seven excellent universities have been established by Swiss cantons and remain under their exclusive control: Basle, Berne, Fribourg, Geneva, Lausanne, Neuchâtel, and Zurich. St. Gallen has created a School of Economics and Public Administration. If these universities should prove inadequate, however, or if their standards should fall, the way is clear for the federal government to step in.

The other method of keeping federalism alive is the Swiss procedure of giving the cantons a very large role in the administration and execution of federal laws. One example is Article 20, which lays down the fundamental rule that: "Federal law shall determine the organiza-

[14] For a discussion of the events leading up to this amendment, see Hughes, pp. 28–29.

tion of the army," followed by: "Execution of laws within the cantons is undertaken by the cantonal authorities, within the limits fixed by federal legislation, and under the supervision of the Confederation." Another is Article 40, which provides:

The system of weights and measures shall be determined by the confederation.

The laws relating thereto shall be carried out by the cantons under the supervision of the Confederation.

An even better example is the division of authority between the federal government and the cantons on criminal law. In 1898 the power to establish a single criminal law for all of Switzerland was given to the federal government, but it was also decided that: "The organization of the judiciary, legal procedure and the administration of justice remain vested in the cantons as in the past."[15] Thus, while there is a single Swiss penal code, created by the federal legislature, the courts that enforce the code remain cantonal as do the organization and procedure of those courts. In principle, the prisons also remain cantonal. This device of leaving the primary responsibility for administration of federal laws in the hands of the cantons permits the increase of federal power without unduly arousing the ire of the federalists (cantonal rights advocates) of which there are still many.

Despite devices and ruses one is forced to the conclusion that the power of the Swiss federal government has increased tremendously over the years, and the end is not yet in sight. On the other hand, federalism is still an important principle in the Swiss political system and will continue to be one for many years to come. The three major factors tending to conserve federalism in Switzerland enumerated by Professor Brooks forty years ago are still valid today. First, each canton is a center of a very active political life of its own. Second, the cantons have as defensive measures the initiative and the referendum, equal representation in the upper house of the federal legislature, and the cantonal basis of party organization. Finally, "they may rely for protection upon the soberness and moderation of the Swiss political character."[16]

Civil Rights

Inasmuch as the Swiss federal state owed its creation largely to the liberal movement in the 1830's and 1840's, the framers of the Federal Constitution were careful to include a number of provisions designed

[15] Art. 64.
[16] Brooks, p. 62.

to protect the Swiss citizen against future arbitrary action on the part of the cantons. Although the Constitution does not include a separate bill of rights, some two dozen articles scattered throughout the general provisions deal with the rights of individuals. These rights are elaborated in great detail. Not only are they defined as well as asserted, but in many cases the corresponding duties of the individual are also set forth.

Since a religious conflict was the immediate cause of the Sonderbund War, and since the anti-clerical authorities were victorious, the drafters of the 1848 Constitution took particular pains to protect the individual, and by inference the state, from the consequences of arbitrary action on the part of organized religions in conjunction with cantonal authorities. The Swiss anti-clericalism of the 1870's, a reaction against dogmatism springing from the development of scientific thought, brought about a further increase in provisions dealing with religion when the Constitution was revised in 1874.

The rights of the Swiss citizen, both those guaranteed by the federal Constitution and others guaranteed by his cantonal constitution, are protected by the courts against infringement by any cantonal authority. This protection can include an appeal to the Federal Tribunal which is the highest court in the land. In practice such appeals are numerous, especially those concerned with a violation of the general right of "equality before the law." This chapter will only describe these rights. The mechanics of protection will be treated later in Chapter 7.

Swiss Citizenship

Citizenship in Switzerland has a threefold basis: communal, cantonal, and federal. A person cannot be a Swiss citizen without being a citizen of a canton and a person cannot be a cantonal citizen without being a citizen of a commune. Neither the revised Constitution of 1874 nor the Constitution of 1848 contains a complete definition of Swiss citizenship, only the provision that: "Every citizen of a canton is a Swiss citizen."[17] Cantonal constitutions pass the responsibility to the lower level by providing that every citizen must also be a citizen of a commune.

In practice communal citizenship, and thus Swiss citizenship, follows a modified rule of *jus sanguinis*. Children born of Swiss parents are automatically citizens of the *father's* commune of origin. A woman who marries a Swiss from another commune loses her original communal citizenship at the time of the marriage and becomes a citizen of

[17] Art. 43 of the Constitution of 1874 and Art. 42 of the Constitution of 1848.

her husband's commune of origin. While a child whose father is a Swiss citizen automatically becomes a Swiss citizen and a citizen of his father's commune and canton, the child born of parents whose mother only is a Swiss citizen does not always acquire Swiss citizenship. The Swiss do not recognize the principle of *jus soli*.

Swiss citizenship can also be acquired by naturalization. Originally, the procedure to be followed and the fee to be paid varied not only from canton to canton but also from commune to commune within each canton. Abuse of the right to grant citizenship by many communes during World War I — almost anyone with the necessary fortune could purchase immediate citizenship in one of the poorer communes — brought federal intervention. Federal legislation of the 1920's, for instance, standardized the classification of persons who were not eligible for citizenship and set twelve years as the minimum length of residence before a foreigner could petition for communal citizenship. Further, federal authorities were given the right to disapprove any individual grant of citizenship.[18]

In principle, Swiss citizenship is also inalienable. Almost no action on the part of a Swiss citizen can automatically deprive him of his citizenship, and the government is expressly forbidden by the Constitution from expelling a Swiss citizen from the country. The exceptions to this rule are few. During World War II, emergency legislation gave the government the exceptional right to deprive of their citizenship Swiss citizens having two or more nationalities if that fact could be construed to be a danger to Swiss neutrality. Further, ordinary legislation of 1952 provides that second generation Swiss born abroad do not automatically become Swiss citizens. In a like manner, a Swiss woman, if she marries a foreigner, may lose her citizenship unless she makes a declaration before marriage that she wishes to retain it.

Freedom of Movement

In general, every Swiss citizen has the right to live anywhere he pleases within the confines of the Confederation. The exceptions to the rule, however, make this right much less complete than it is in the United States, for instance. The canton in which an individual wishes to settle can require that he produce a "certificate of origin" or some

[18] Cantons are free to set standards within the limits imposed by federal legislation. While some cantons have set minimal standards, most now make it quite difficult to become a Swiss citizen. Recently, for instance, an individual of Chinese extraction who had resided in the commune of Berne for twenty-five years had his application for citizenship rejected primarily on the basis that he had failed to become sufficiently part of the community.

similar identifying document from his commune of origin. The commune of origin may decline to issue such a certificate, or another commune may decline to release it, under certain conditions such as the non-payment of particular taxes.

Even with a certificate of origin the right to reside may be limited. Permission may be refused in cases where the person in question has been deprived of his civil rights as a consequence of a criminal judgment. Further, the right to reside may be withdrawn by another canton in cases where an individual has been "repeatedly sentenced for grave misdemeanors" or has "become a permanent burden upon public charity" and to whom the canton or commune of origin refused adequate assistance after having been officially requested to render it.[19] In no case, however, is the canton of origin permitted to refuse a Swiss citizen the right to return.

In view of the right of cantons to withdraw the privilege to reside from those who become a permanent charge on public charity, the responsibility for the care of indigent Swiss citizens always falls ultimately on his canton of origin. To eliminate many of the legal and procedural difficulties that have arisen as more and more Swiss reside outside of their cantons of origin, a group of cantons drafted and signed an intercantonal concordat to provide for relief at the place of domicile. This agreement, which came into force in 1920 and was revised in 1923 and 1937, provides that the cost of relief shall be shared between the place of origin and the place of domicile according to a proportion based upon the length of time the pauper has resided outside the canton of origin. By 1955 seventeen and a half cantons had accepted the agreement.

It is interesting to note that a provision of the 1848 Constitution, dropped in a revision of 1866, granted the freedom of settlement only to those of a "Christian faith" supplied with (1) a certificate of origin, (2) a certificate of good moral character, and (3) an attestation that the bearer undertook his civil responsibilities and was not legally dishonored.[20]

Equality Before the Law

According to Article 4 of the Swiss Federal Constitution, "All Swiss are equal before the law." This is further amplified in the same article by the statement that: "In Switzerland there are neither subjects nor privileges of rank, birth, person, or family." Article 60 adds: "Every canton is obliged to accord to citizens of other confederate states the

[19] Art. 45.
[20] Art. 41 of the 1848 Constitution.

same treatment it accords to its own citizens, as regards legislation and all that concerns judicial proceedings."[21]

The Constitution further guarantees that no person may be deprived of his lawful judge and abolishes ecclesiastical courts. In the eyes of the framers of the Constitution, these provisions were necessary to eliminate the creation of *ad hoc* courts such as those used for the persecution of the Liberals during the Sonderbund War and to keep ecclesiastical courts out of civil affairs. The provision regarding a citizen's lawful judge "is now only used against *arbitrariness* in sending people to one tribunal rather than to another or in refusing jurisdiction."[22] Personal claims against a "solvent debtor" must be brought before the courts of the debtor's place of residence, but valid judgments in civil cases rendered in one canton can be executed anywhere on Swiss territory. Imprisonment for civil debt is not permitted in Switzerland.

As concerns criminal matters, the Constitution prohibits corporal punishment and the death penalty for a political crime. A provision of the 1874 constitutional revision abolished the death penalty for other causes, but it was reintroduced in 1878 as a result of a constitutional amendment. Several cantons, Appenzell-Inner Rhodes, Obwalden, Uri, Schwyz, Zug, St. Gallen, Lucerne, Valais, Schaffhausen, and Fribourg, hastened to avail themselves of the right. As long as the cantons were responsible for their own criminal codes, there was nothing that the federal government could do. This situation was changed, however, when the federal government was authorized to legislate on criminal law. The Federal Criminal Code, which came into force in 1942, reestablishes the prohibition on capital punishment except for serious crimes committed in times of war and during active military service.[23]

Freedom of Press, Association and Petition

The freedom of the press is guaranteed throughout Switzerland with the proviso that cantonal legislatures may enact "measures necessary for the repression of abuses," and the federal government "has the right to prescribe penalties in order to suppress abuses directed against itself or its authorities."[24] All cantonal laws directed against the abuse of the press must be submitted to the Federal Council for its approval. In general, however, the press is controlled by the federal Criminal Code

[21] For a discussion of the application of Art. 4 in court proceedings, see Hughes, pp. 6–8.

[22] Hughes, p. 71.

[23] See G. Sauser-Hall, *The Political Institutions of Switzerland* (Zurich: Swiss National Tourist Office, 1946), pp. 79–80.

[24] Art. 55.

which contains repressive measures to combat libel, slander, and other such abuses. The scope of the control that the federal government can exercise is fairly wide, especially where Swiss international relations are involved. In times of war between neighboring countries, freedom of the press in Switzerland has been restricted quite severely. Restrictions have been extended to film and radio, and the penalties have included confiscation and suppression. In practice, in peacetime, the Swiss have very few occasions to use restrictive legislation. The Swiss press is highly responsible and conservative, rarely engaging in the "sensationalism" that is a characteristic of many newspapers in the United States.

The Swiss are also guaranteed the freedom of association and petition. The freedom of association has been interpreted to include the formation of organized groups for religious, political, social, and economic aims and to include the right of assembly. This right is subject, however, to the provision that neither the purpose of the association nor the means it employs are in any way "unlawful or dangerous to the State."[25] As concerns the right of petition, it should be noted that the competent Swiss officials make an effort to take most petitions seriously, but the right itself has lost a great deal of importance as a result of the adoption of the constitutional initiative.

Freedom of Religion

The two basic provisions of the Swiss Constitution dealing with freedom of religion are, first, paragraph 1 of Article 50, which reads: "The free exercise of forms of worship is guaranteed within the limits compatible with public order and decency." And, second, paragraph 1 of Article 49, which states: "Liberty of conscience and belief is inviolable." The latter is reinforced by the provision that: (1) "No person may be compelled to become a member of any religious body, to submit to any religious instruction, to perform any religious act, or to incur any punishment of any sort by reason of religious opinion." (2) "No person may be compelled to pay taxes the proceeds of which are devoted specifically to pay the expenses of the ritual of any religious community of which he is not a member." And (3), "The exercise of civil or political rights may not be limited by religious or ecclesiastical requirements or conditions of any nature."

There are certain general conditions attached to the freedom of religion, however. A father is expressly given the right to determine what type of religious education a child shall receive up to that child's sixteenth birthday, and no one may be released from the per-

25 Art. 56.

formance of his civil duties by reason of his religious beliefs. The latter provision has been used to punish conscientious objectors for refusing to do their military service. The "public order and decency" clause of Article 50 was used at one time to curtail the noise-making activities of the Salvation Army.

There are also a variety of more specific restrictions placed on religious practices by the framers of the 1848 Constitution and reinforced by the revisions of 1874, most of which were aimed directly at the Catholic church and the Jesuits in particular. As concerns the latter, Article 51 states expressly that: "The Order of Jesuits and societies affiliated thereto may not be admitted in any part of Switzerland and their members are forbidden to take any part in the activities of any church or school." The subordinate clause was added in 1874 in order to make the prohibition applicable to individual activity as well as organized activity. The 1874 revision also added the provision that: "The founding of new convents or religious orders, and the re-establishment of those which have been suppressed, are forbidden."[26]

Among the provisions in the Constitution aimed at curbing former practices of the Catholic church in general is that of placing the "right to marry" under the protection of the Confederation. As a result of Article 54, inserted in the Constitution in 1874, the civil ceremony of marriage is the only one legal in the eyes of the law. Further: "No bar to marriage may be based upon grounds of religious belief, the poverty of one or other of the partners, their past conduct, or from any other consideration of public policy." Illegitimate children are legitimized by the subsequent marriage of their parents. The 1874 revision also took records of births, deaths, and marriages out of the hands of the clergy and placed them in the hands of the civil authorities. Cemeteries, where there had been conflict in the past over the right of non-church members to be buried, were also placed in the care of civil authorities, and every one was guaranteed a decent burial. It is also interesting to note that no new bishoprics may be set up on Swiss territory without the consent of the federal authorities. The purpose of this provision was to eliminate the possibility of foreign bishops gaining authority over sections of Switzerland, a situation which had led to difficulties in the past in Ticino.

The Swiss Constitution also grants the federal government powers to handle almost any other situation that might arise. In addition to the competence that is inherent in the provisions already cited, Article 50 states: "The cantons and the Confederation may take the measures necessary to maintain public order and peace between members of

[26] Art. 52.

different religious communities, and to prevent the encroachments by ecclesiastical authorities upon the rights of citizens and of the State." In addition: "Disputes within the sphere of public or private law arising out of the creation of religious communities, or a schism of existing ones, may be brought before the competent federal authorities." As if the powers of the federal government over unwanted religious activity were not already complete, the 1874 revision added to the article prohibiting the activities of the Jesuits the following provision: "This prohibition may be extended, by federal decree, to other religious orders whose activity is dangerous to the State or disturbs the peaceable relationship of religious denominations."[27]

Odd as it may seem to the American observer, nevertheless the majority of cantons have recognized state churches (called National Churches). The canton organizes these churches, supports them entirely from special taxes or grants them regular subsidies, and confers on them privileges that other churches do not enjoy. Furthermore, in some cantons the clergy of the state church are classed as cantonal officials and paid out of cantonal funds. This system is in force in most of the Protestant cantons and in a great number of Catholic cantons.

Several other Catholic cantons operate under the "concordat system" in which the Pope or Bishops negotiate a concordat with the civil authorities which defines the rights and duties of the two parties with regard to the churches in that canton. A few cantons, on the other hand, have adopted a system of separation of church and state, also called the "American system." In these cantons the state has given up any attempt to organize the churches and leaves them free to do as they wish. Separation of the church and state has existed in Geneva since 1907, and, in a modified form, in Basle since 1910. The regime under which the Catholic Church operates in Ticino is close to being a system of separation, although the cantonal constitution identifies the Catholic religion as the cantonal religion.

In some seventeen cantons there is a special tax, the proceeds from which are used to support the state churches. These taxes are real and enforceable. In order for the tax to be legal under Article 49 mentioned above, provisions are made to the effect that individuals can be relieved of the tax burden by publicly and formally denying that they adhere to the state religion or by renouncing religion altogether. Many of the more liberal Swiss consider that this procedure places an undue burden, moral at least, on the person who does not believe that a state tax should be used to support any particular religion. As one Swiss

[27] Art. 51, para. 2.

writer has observed, it amounts to "pay or get out."[28] Furthermore, as pointed out by Christopher Hughes, in some cases non-members of the congregation "can be constrained to pay that part of the Church rate which is not devoted 'specially' to religious purposes — they must pay their share of such things as the upkeep of the churchyard, belfry, and clock."[29]

[28] Henry Babel, *Journal de Genève* (April 11, 1960), 2.
[29] Hughes, p. 63.

Democracy

Switzerland is often thought of as the most democratic of modern state systems. To a large extent it is. No other country relies so heavily upon the modern instruments of direct democracy — the initiative and the referendum. In the first place, all constitutional amendments, no matter what their source, must receive the approval of a majority of voters. Secondly, the people themselves have been given the power to initiate changes in the Constitution. The voter is not limited to approval or disapproval of proposals offered by the federal legislature. Finally, and this is where the "democratic" label assumes special significance, the people are given the constitutional right to force the federal authorities to submit most major legislation and important treaties for popular approval. When one includes in one's consideration similar rights in most cantonal and communal matters, the Swiss voter truly becomes an essential part of the legislative process.

On the other hand, Switzerland can be labeled as one of the least democratic of modern democratic systems. This contradiction lies in the fact that Switzerland is the only important nation in Europe, and one of the few remaining in the world, that refuses women the right to vote on national affairs and on most local questions. Thus, while the Swiss male has a greater role in the democratic process than his counterpart anywhere — if one includes cantonal and communal matters he is at times called to the polls as often as once a month — the Swiss woman has a lesser role.

This chapter will begin with a discussion of the qualifications for voting in Switzerland and the problem of woman suffrage, and then will take up the three types of direct democracy at the federal level: (1) the compulsory referendum on constitutional amendments; (2) the popular

1971
△

initiative for proposing constitutional revisions and amendments; and (3) the optional referendum on laws and treaties.

The Right to Vote

Both the federal government and the cantons are responsible for establishing voting qualifications. Although it would seem plausible under these circumstances to give the federal government the responsibility of establishing qualifications for voting on federal issues and to leave to the cantons the responsibility for establishing the qualifications on cantonal matters, such is not the case. Qualifications for voting in the latter are partially under the control of federal law and, in some instances, voting in federal matters is regulated by cantonal law. We are primarily concerned here with the right to vote in federal matters which include elections to the popular house of the federal legislature, the constitutional initiative and referendum, the legislative and treaty referenda and elections to federal juries.

For the right to vote in federal matters, the basic text is Article 74 of the Swiss Constitution which reads:

> Every Swiss aged twenty or more, and not otherwise disqualified for active citizenship by the legislation of the Canton where he has his place of residence, has the right to vote at elections and referenda.
>
> Federal legislation may regulate in a uniform manner the exercise of this right.

If the Swiss federal legislature should use the power given to it in the second paragraph of this article, the problem of overlapping jurisdictions on voting qualifications in federal matters would not arise. It has not done so, however. The one federal law passed under this provision on July 19, 1872, only partially covered the field and expressly left the remainder to cantonal legislation.[1]

In principle, then, the right to vote in federal matters is conferred on all Swiss citizens twenty years of age or older. Although no distinction is made between those who acquired their citizenship by birth and those who acquired it by naturalization, the federal authorities have always interpreted the words of the Constitution, "every Swiss," to refer only to men. While the woman suffrage movement will be discussed later in this section, it will suffice at this juncture to point out that the Federal Council has reaffirmed this interpretation as recently as 1957.

In accordance with the general practice in most democracies, certain

[1] *Loi fédérale du 19 juillet 1872 sur les élections et votations fédérales.*

groups of people can be deprived of voting rights. Here again there is an overlapping of jurisdictions between federal and cantonal authorities. In this case, however, the former has at least attempted to use its power to eliminate the discrepancies. Article 66 of the Constitution provides that: "Federal legislation shall determine the circumstances in which a Swiss citizen may be deprived of his political rights." On two occasions, 1874 and 1877, federal laws were passed to bring some sort of uniformity in the matter. On both occasions the people rejected them in referenda. In 1882, a draft law from the Federal Council on the same subject was rejected by the federal legislature before it even got to the people.

Neverthless, federal and cantonal laws have established three general types of cases where a male Swiss citizen of twenty years of age or over can be deprived of his right to vote: (1) In most cantons a person can be deprived of his civic rights if found to be mentally incompetent. (2) The Swiss Criminal Code provides that a person can be deprived of his right to vote if found guilty of certain serious crimes. In Switzerland this deprivation can be continued, under certain circumstances, after release from a penal institution.[2] And (3), in most cantons a voter can lose his voting rights as a result of bankruptcy. Some cantons have fixed additional reasons for the deprivation of the right, such as: when a person has become a public charge through his own fault; when a person has accepted service under a foreign power; and when a person has been forbidden entry into public inns because of habitual drunkenness.[3]

Voting procedure does not differ radically from that in most democracies. Voting dates for federal matters are fixed by the federal authorities or by federal law in all cases except elections to federal juries and special elections to the federal legislature. Then the responsibility belongs to cantonal authorities. As a general rule electors vote in their place of residence. Nevertheless, members of the Federal Council, the Chancellor of the Confederation and members of the Federal Tribunal exercise their civic rights in their commune of origin no matter where they actually reside. Men doing their military service vote where they are stationed for federal questions and at their place of residence for cantonal and communal matters. As mentioned earlier, a person who moves from one canton to another can exercise his right to vote in federal matters immediately upon arrival and registration. Cantons provide the electoral register in which the voter's name must

[2] See *Code pénal suisse du 21 décembre 1937*, Art. 52.
[3] See Marcel Bridel, *Précis de Droit constitutionnel et public suisse, 2eme Partie: Les Organes de l'État* (Lausanne: Payot, 1959), p. 34.

be inscribed, and in most cases the voter must present a registration card to vote. Cantonal authorities are responsible for notifying voters of elections and the results of elections, and for providing polling places and the necessary voting officials. Federal law provides that voting must be secret, forbids voting by proxy, and makes federal crimes of certain actions, such as a violation of the secret ballot and preventing people by force from voting.

Several cantons have made voting obligatory. In some it is obligatory in all elections, in a few only for cantonal elections, and in others only for federal matters. In some cases there is a nominal fine for non-voting, in others no fine is fixed. Among those which make voting in federal matters obligatory and attach a fine, are Schaffhausen, St. Gallen, Aargau, and Thurgau.[4]

As mentioned earlier, women do not have the right to vote in Swiss federal matters. The woman suffrage movement has been active in Switzerland for many years, however, and recently there have been some successes on the cantonal level. For a long time this movement made no headway. On the federal level, two motions introduced into the legislature in 1918 to grant women the same civic rights as men were ignored. In 1929 a petition to grant women the right to vote, signed by about 250,000 people, was deposited in Berne, but no action was taken on it by the legislature. Although the Federal Council accepted a postulate in December, 1945, calling for a partial revision of the Constitution "in order to express publicly the confidence we have in our Swiss women," the Council of States refused, in 1951, to permit the Federal Council to draw up a constitutional amendment for submission to the people. The suffrage movement did not progress on the cantonal level either. On nineteen occasions, between 1919 and 1954, initiatives to revise cantonal constitutions to allow women to vote were turned down by referendum. Several other attempts on the cantonal level fell through even before reaching the voting stage. Although the feminist movement had gained many professional rights for women over these same years, nothing had been accomplished on the political level except to gain voting rights in certain cantons on such things as ecclesiastical and educational matters.[5]

The events that finally led to the granting of woman suffrage in the

---

[4] For a discussion of voting in cantonal matters, as opposed to federal matters, see Bridel, pp. 38–45.

[5] See Sauser-Hall, *Guide politique suisse,* pp. 116–117. In 1958, the women of Basle Town with Basle citizenship were given the right to vote in certain communal matters under the jurisdiction of the local burgers, mostly as concerns the administration of welfare funds.

cantons of Vaud, Neuchâtel, and Geneva, in 1959 and 1960, were set in motion by the Federal Council. In a message accompanying the decision of 1957 that Article 74 of the Constitution granted the vote only to Swiss men, the Federal Council put itself on record to the effect that it was desirable to grant equal political rights to women. The Swiss Federal legislature agreed on June 13, 1958, and on February 1, 1959, a constitutional amendment to give the voting right to women was submitted to the male electorate. The proposal was turned down by a vote of more than two to one, 654,924 to 323,306.

Although the action of the male voters in 1959 resulted in keeping the status quo on the federal level, it precipitated a change in three cantons. In the first place, the canton of Vaud had voted simultaneously on granting women suffrage on the cantonal level. The proposal was successful by a majority of 32,947 to 31,252. The two other cantons that had voted in favor of the 1959 amendment — Geneva, where the vote was 17,755 to 11,842 and Neuchâtel, where it was 13,938 to 12,755 — held new referenda. The male voters of Neuchâtel granted women the right to vote on September 29, 1959, by a majority of 11,240 to 9,738. On March 6, 1960, the Geneva males also agreed by a vote of 18,119 to 14,624.[6]

While victory of the feminists in Vaud, Neuchâtel, and Geneva does not mean that the whole of Switzerland will immediately reverse the verdict of February 1, 1959, it is a portent for the future. The three French-speaking cantons have often been in the forefront of liberal movements that later have been adopted by other cantons. If past performances is any criterion, the feminists will next concentrate their attention on the cantons which came close to granting women suffrage in the 1959 referendum, such as Basle Town where the vote was 47 per cent in the affirmative, and other areas usually known for their progressive attitudes. Zurich and Berne are good possibilities. Once the major cantons get behind the movement there is a good chance that the others will follow suit, at least enough to carry the next national referendum. Some of the more conservative cantons, such as Schwyz, where the men voted ten to one against the 1959 proposal, may never of their own accord grant women the right to vote.

Despite the recent advances, it still seems odd that Switzerland with

[6] The first women to be elected to public office as a result of these decisions included several members of communal councils, one vice-president of a commune, and a member of a cantonal parliament. The latter was Miss Raymonde Schweizer of La Chaux-de-Fonds, who was elected in 1960 to the Neuchâtel Grand Council. The women of Geneva participated in their first cantonal referendum on December 4, 1960.

its liberal democratic heritage should be one of the last countries to refuse women the right to vote. The old argument that perhaps the women do not want to vote was put to rest when two cantons gave their women the chance to make their preference known. In a 1953 consultation, the Genevese women answered in the affirmative by 36,000 to 6,000, and in 1954 the women of Basle Town agreed by 33,000 to 12,000.[7] The standard arguments used, in 1959 and 1960, that it would not only coarsen women to be involved in politics but also turn them away from their duties to children, kitchen, and church, ignores the experience of the majority of the world. It is also argued that the resulting increase in the electorate would mean the end of the *Landsgemeinde*. Nevertheless, although most of the arguments of the Swiss males are illogical, the fact remains that women still do not have any suffrage on either federal or cantonal matters in eighteen and a half cantons, and will probably continue to be deprived of this right for many years to come.

Direct Democracy

Compulsory Constitutional Referendum

All changes in the Swiss Federal Constitution must be approved in a national referendum by a majority of all votes cast and by a majority of the cantons. This process is known as the compulsory constitutional referendum. Referenda can be initiated by the federal legislature or by the people through a petition, and the proposed revision can be partial or total. This section will treat the general topic of compulsory constitutional referendum and the legislative method of proposing changes. The popular initiative will be discussed in the following section.

The constitutional referendum in its modern form originated in the United States and came to Switzerland with the French Act of Mediation in 1803. It was discarded under the Pact of 1815 but reintroduced in several cantons during the revolutionary movements of the 1830's. It was introduced in its present form in the 1848 Constitution and first used when the Constitution itself was submitted to the approval of the people and the cantons.

As mentioned above, constitutional amendments may be total or partial. The legislature may initiate either type by the ordinary process of legislative action. The Federal Council may draw up a proposal which is then submitted to the two houses for independent deliberation, or one of the two houses may start the process. If the houses agree

[7] See Sauser-Hall, *Guide . . .*, p. 117.

on a text it is submitted to the people on the next convenient date. As stated before, the amendment takes effect only if it receives the approval of a majority of Swiss citizens voting on it and a majority of cantons. The vote of each canton is determined by the majority of the vote within its territory. For the determining of the overall cantonal vote, a half-canton is considered as a half-vote. Thus an amendment must receive a majority of all the votes cast and a majority in at least 11½ cantons.

In general, constitutional amendments proposed by the legislature have been frequent and successful. In the 115-year period from 1848 to 1963 the legislature proposed seventy-nine amendments, of which fifty-four have been accepted by the people and the cantons.[8]

Two points in regard to a total revision should be mentioned. In the initiating stage, the Constitution provides that if agreement cannot be reached between the two houses on a single text, either house may take the question of a general revision to the people. This is done by passing a resolution to the effect that the Constitution should be totally revised. The people are then requested to vote yes or no. (The cantonal vote is not counted in this case.) If the answer is negative the problem is ended. If, on the other hand, a majority of the people vote affirmatively, the legislature is dissolved, and new elections are held. The new legislature shall then "take in hand the work of total revision."[9] This has never occurred in Swiss experience. In fact, total revision by legislative proposal has been attempted only twice: once, in 1872, when it was refused by the people; and again in 1874, when it was accepted. Both times the two houses were in agreement on a text. There is a fair possibility that it may be attempted again, however. There seems to be a growing feeling in Switzerland that the Constitution should be entirely redrafted in order to eliminate the confusion that exists as a result of the numerous partial amendments (some articles have up to four additions), to eliminate certain articles that no longer have any real validity, and in general to create a basic instrument more adapted to the times.

Constitutional Initiative

The popular constitutional initiative, included in the Constitutions of 1848 and 1874, was also an outgrowth of cantonal practice which had originated in the liberal movement of the 1830's. It did not come into

[8] Rappard, *The Government of Switzerland,* p. 70, and *Annuaire statistique de la Suisse, 1947,* pp. 480–481; *1953,* pp. 510–511; *1959/1960,* pp. 530–531; and *1963,* pp. 538–539.

[9] Art. 120.

general use, however, until a clarifying amendment was added to the Constitution in 1891.

Before 1891, the Constitution simply stated that a constitutional amendment could be initiated by a petition of 50,000 registered voters. Another provision of the early Constitutions stated that the people must first be requested to vote on the general question of whether the Constitution should be revised. If the people answered in the affirmative, the legislature had to be dissolved and new elections held. The Constitution did not specify whether this procedure referred to a total revision, partial revision, or both.

In 1880, a petition with 50,000 signatures was deposited with the federal legislature requesting a partial amendment to give the federal government a bank note monopoly. After deliberation, the legislature came to the conclusion that the popular initiative could be used only to initiate a total constitutional revision. The legislature then posed the question to the people of whether a total revision was then desired and noted that if their answer was in the affirmative, the two legislative houses would be dissolved and new elections held. On October 31, 1880, the people answered negatively by a vote of 260,126 to 121,099.[10] Agitation was begun immediately for a constitutional amendment to provide specifically for partial revisions by means of the popular initiative without the consequences of a total revision. In 1891 the movement gained its objective when the legislature initiated and the people accepted such an amendment.

As it now stands, the Swiss Constitution provides for both total and partial revision on the petition of 50,000 Swiss citizens who are entitled to vote. If the petition is for total revision, and the people accept, the consequences are as before. Since 1891 there has been only one proposal for a total revision, in 1935. It was defeated.

The 1891 amendment provides that petitioners can present requests for a partial revision either in general terms or in the form of a completed text. In the former case, if the legislature agrees with the suggestion, it proceeds to draft a constitutional amendment in accordance with the sense expressed in the petition and submits it to popular and cantonal vote. If the legislature should disagree with the suggestion, then the project is submitted to a referendum. If a majority of the people insist (the cantons are not counted in this procedure), the legislature must work out a project along the lines of the wish expressed and submit it to a popular and cantonal referendum.

If the petitioners present a draft text, the procedure is slightly different. As occurs in the previous case, the petition is first given to the

[10] See Rappard, *La Constitution fédérale de la Suisse,* pp. 294–298.

Federal Chancellery to check the validity of the signatures. Not only must the signatures be those of registered voters, but they must have been collected within a period of six months before submission of the petition. If the petition is found to be valid, it is turned over to the legislature for action. The legislature has three courses to follow: if in agreement with the project, it submits it to a popular and cantonal referendum; if in disagreement, it can submit the proposed text to a referendum along with a recommendation to reject it; or it can submit both a counterproject and the original text to a referendum. The enabling act provides that if the legislature fails to reach a decision, it must in any case submit the project to the people and the cantons within three years of its receipt from the Federal Chancellery.[11]

From 1874 to 1963 some forty-eight initiatives were submitted, seven of which the people accepted. The legislature has used its prerogative to submit counterproposals nine times; six times the counterproposals were accepted by the people. There has been a steady increase in the use of the initiative, although no corresponding increases in acceptances.

Legislative Referendum

In its search for popular democracy, the Swiss have also resorted to the legislative referendum. Adopted for cantonal use in the 1830's, the legislative referendum was made a part of the federal Constitution in 1874. It differs from the procedure for popular alteration of the Constitution in two respects. First, there is no provision for initiating legislation by popular petition, only for referring legislation already passed by the legislature to the people. Attempts in the past to introduce a legislative initiative have always failed. Second, the rejection of a piece of legislation does not require a majority of cantons, only a popular majority. The reason for the differences in procedure is simple. If a majority of cantons were also required, there would be no fundamental difference from the requirements for amending the constitution.

The procedure is as follows. Article 89 of the Constitution provides that all federal laws and "universally binding *arrêtés*" must be submitted to the people on demand of 30,000 Swiss citizens entitled to vote or of eight cantons.[12] Such a petition or demand by eight cantons

[11] Hughes, *The Federal Constitution of Switzerland,* p. 136.

[12] In Swiss practice there is little difference in either form or substance between a law and an *arrêté.* As will be explained below, the major difference, in practice, is that *arrêtés* can, under certain circumstances, be exempt from legislative referenda. A discussion of ordinances of the federal executive, also called *arrêtés,* will be undertaken in the chapter dealing with the executive branch of the government.

must be received within ninety days after the official publication of the law or *arrêté*. If the demand is made within the time limit, a day is set for the referendum, and the law or *arrêté* is considered rejected when a majority votes negatively.

As a general rule all laws must be submitted to the legislative referendum. The constitutional provision concerning *arrêtés*, on the other hand, includes an escape clause. *Arrêtés* determined by the legislature to be "urgent" or "not universally binding" are exempt from popular challenge. While a declaration of "urgent" requires an affirmative vote of the majority of all the members of both houses of legislature, an *arrêté* is usually made "not universally binding" by simply not providing it with a referendum clause. Since the legislature has no desire to have its work interrupted too often by popular interference, a majority of legislation is designated as *arrêtés* rather than laws, and most of the former are declared "urgent" or "not universally binding."

In an attempt to curb an abuse of this practice, frequently used during the unsettled 1930's and 1940's, a popular initiative dubbed the "Initiative for the Return to Direct Democracy" was accepted by the people in September, 1949. Incorporated as Article 89 *bis* of the Constitution, it provides that "urgent" universally binding *arrêtés* go out of force after one year if challenged by a legislative referendum and are not sanctioned. It provides further that legislative *arrêtés* which "infringe the Constitution" must be sanctioned by both the people and the cantons in the year following their adoption by the legislature. If not, they automatically go out of force at the end of the one year period and cannot be re-enacted. Although still too early to determine what effects this initiative will have on legislation, its introduction tends to prove that the democratic traditions of the Swiss are still alive.

The most recent addition to the Swiss direct democratic procedures is the optional treaty referendum. At first disapproved by the federal legislature, and then postponed by World War I, it was accepted by the people on January 30, 1921.[13] Paragraph 3 of Article 89 provides: "International treaties concluded for an unlimited duration or for more than fifteen years shall also be submitted to the people for acceptance or rejection if demanded by 30,000 Swiss citizens entitled to vote, or eight cantons." The optional treaty referendum was used in February, 1923, when the Swiss voters rejected a French treaty that would have abolished the customs-free zones surrounding Geneva,

[13] This approval occurred one-half year after the Swiss legislature had voluntarily asked the people whether Switzerland should become a member of the League of Nations.

and in 1958 when they approved an Italian treaty providing for the use of part of the Swiss National Park in the Spöl for a hydroelectric project.

The legislative referendum, in general, has been used some 70 times since its adoption, and in only 26 cases have the voters given their approval.

Direct Democracy in Action

Some observations concerning the use to which the Swiss have put their system of direct democracy are in order at this point. In the first place, they have been called upon to use their system often, almost 200 times since 1848. On an overall basis, this is about 1.7 times a year. There has been an increase over the years, however, as shown by Professor Rappard in 1936: the average number of plebiscites between 1848 and 1874 was 0.4 times a year, increasing to 1.5 between the adoption of the Constitution in 1874 and World War I, and jumping to 2.4 between 1914 and 1935.[14] Since 1935 the frequency of referenda increased to approximately 2.8 times a year. In the second and third periods under observation by Professor Rappard, the increase was due in large part to the introduction of new methods of direct democracy, the constitutional initiative and the optional legislative referendum. The increase in the third period, and the period from 1935 to the present may be due mainly to the increased age of the Constitution as a whole.

As concerns the degree of participation, it varies greatly according to the issue before the electorate. In the ten-year period from January 1, 1950, to January 1, 1960, for instance, the average turnout was 50.4 per cent, rising to a maximum of 66.7 per cent on the constitutional referendum concerning voting rights for women and dropping to a minimum of 37.6 per cent on a popular intiative to regulate business. The former was accepted and the latter rejected. The turnout also varies greatly from canton to canton. In the 1959 referendum on woman suffrage the average turnout was 66.7 per cent, with a high of 86.6 per cent in Schaffhausen and a low of 45.0 per cent in Geneva. It is interesting to note that the turnout in those cantons with compulsory voting and fines for not voting is consistently high. In the 1959 referendum the four cantons mentioned earlier, Schaffhausen, Aargau, Thurgau, and St. Gallen, provided four of the five highest percentages, or 86.6, 84.9, 78.6, and 75 respectively.

As might be expected, the Swiss are much more likely to accept a suggestion to change the Constitution emanating from the legislature

[14] Rappard, *The Government of Switzerland,* p. 71.

than from a popular petition. Since it was introduced in 1848, about 67 per cent of all legislative proposals have been accepted in referendum. In the period 1935 to 1960, for example, only eight out of twenty-six proposed changes were rejected. Popular initiatives, on the other hand, have had a consistently hard time at the voters' hands. Almost 90 per cent of all such proposals have been turned down. In the 1935 to 1960 period, a particularly difficult one for the popular initiative, only one was accepted out of twenty. The few counter-proposals that the legislature has taken the trouble to submit have fared much better. Three out of the five submitted by the legislature from 1935 to 1960 were approved.

The Swiss have also found use for the optional legislative referendum. About 63 per cent of all pieces of legislation that have found their way to the people have been rejected. It should be remembered, however, that by reason of the limits established by the Constitution or the legislative interpretation of the constitutional provisions, only a very small portion of all legislation is ever subject to the legislative referendum. It is also still true that "the fear of popular repudiation is often a more potent factor in preventing the adoption by Parliament of certain legislative measures than the actual repudiation itself."[15]

A basic conservatism in governmental affairs is evident in the manner in which the Swiss voter assumes the responsibility for direct democracy. First, although he prefers to have changes in the Constitution proposed by the federal legislature, rather than by petition, the popular initiative is considered to be an essential right. Second, many proposals to amend the Constitution, no matter from what source, must be submitted to the referendum several times before ultimate approval. Very few basic changes have been made in the Swiss Constitution on the first try. Third, the proposals by the popular initiative are usually quite serious. Very few "radical" or frivolous initiatives have been submitted to the referendum. Those that have, such as those offered by certain right-wing political groups just before World War II, were rejected by substantial majorities.

More Direct Democracy?

The Swiss have not necessarily exhausted all the possibilities for direct democracy; there still remains the popular legislative initiative on the federal level. The Radical party, one of the three most important Swiss political parties, has constantly advocated the introduction of the legislative initiative and recently it has been joined by the Socialists.

[15] *Ibid.,* p. 72.

Further, all cantons have provisions in their constitutions for the popular initiation of laws; the roots of this procedure can also be found in the liberal movements of the 1830's.[16]

The arguments for the institution of the legislative initiative on the federal level are varied. It is argued that it would demonstrate more fully the confidence that the nation has in the integrity of the average Swiss voter, that it would increase the sense of participation of the voter in federal affairs, and that it is a right that the voter is entitled to enjoy. Of a more practical nature, there is the argument that it would eliminate the practice of using the constitutional initiative to insert into the Constitution provisions that should ordinarily be drafted as laws. Article 32 *ter*, which outlaws the manufacture, importation, transportation, or sale of absinthe in Switzerland, is one of the provisions used as an example.[17]

Arguments against the institution of the legislative initiative are also varied. It has been pointed out that it would be considered as a vote of lack of confidence in the representatives of the people, that it is unnecessary in view of the other institutions of direct democracy available to the electorate, and that it would unduly complicate the work of the federal legislature. Perhaps one of the most important arguments heretofore presented against the legislative initiative is that it would further reduce the importance of the cantons and their protection against the encroachment of the federal government. At present no constitutional amendment can become effective without the approval of a majority of the cantons. In ordinary legislation the cantons are protected by the necessity of agreement by the Council of States and, although the legislative referendum requires only the assent of the majority of the electorate, the Council of States still has a hand in the preparation of the law in question.[18] The one time the legislative initiative was presented to the voters, October 22, 1961, the arguments against its introduction were decisive.[19]

---

[16] In the *Landsgemeinde* cantons each individual voter exercises this right directly as a member of the legislative body.

[17] See the arguments presented in the series of articles brought together by the editors of the Radical newspaper *Neue Zürcher Zeitung* in *Grenzen der direkten Demokratie* (Zurich: Buchverlag Neue Zürcher Zeitung, 1959).

[18] See Rappard, pp. 69–70. Rappard also points out that if a majority of the voters and the cantons should be required for approval of a legislative initiative, "the only distinction still existing between constitutional and ordinary legislative measures would disappear."

[19] The proposal was defeated by 409,445 votes to 170,842.

✚ 5 ✚

The Federal Assembly

"Subject to the rights reserved to the people and the cantons, the supreme authority of the Confederation is exercised by the Federal Assembly which is composed of two sections or councils: A. the National Council; B. the Council of States."[1] The legislature is given the power to make all federal laws, and it appoints the members of other major federal bodies and supervises their work. In principle, no other federal body has the power to hinder or nullify the actions of the legislature; the ultimate responsibility for the direction of the Swiss federal government rests in the hands of the representatives of the people and the cantons.

The manner in which the Federal Assembly exercises its responsibilities is an entirely different matter, however. As will become apparent in this chapter and the next, the legislature has come to rely more and more on the seven-man federal executive for leadership. In this process it has given the executive an increasing number of tasks that the framers of the 1848 Constitution felt would normally be the responsibility of the legislature.

Functions

The Federal Assembly has all the normal legislative powers of a parliamentary body. Article 85, Section 1, of the Constitution provides that it has exclusive authority to legislate on all matters not reserved to the cantons. The Constitution, however, differentiates between the passing of laws and *arrêtés*. As mentioned earlier, the difference between the two is a matter of form rather than content. All laws are

[1] Art. 71.

normally subject to the optional legislative referendum. *Arrêtés,* on the other hand, can be exempt from popular challenge if they are not "universally binding" or if they are declared "urgent" by an affirmative vote of the total members of both houses of legislature.[2] As a rule, in order to prevent popular interference with the day-to-day affairs of government, *arrêtés* are much more common than laws. It has been estimated that in the fifty-year period from 1900 to 1950 the annual ratio of legislative *arrêtés* to laws has been on the order of about six to one.[3] Also, as noted earlier, the Federal Assembly has the power to propose amendments to the Constitution.

The federal legislature has broad appointive powers. The Constitution specifically provides that it shall elect the members of the Federal Council, the Federal Tribunal, the Chancellor of the Confederation, and a Commander in Chief in times of emergency. The Constitution also entrusts the legislature not only with the designation of the President and Vice-President of the Federal Council, but also with the right to assume "other rights of election or confirmation."[4] Under this general power, the legislature has taken upon itself the responsibility of appointing the President and Vice-President of the Federal Tribunal and of electing the members of the Federal Insurance Tribunal. Finally, the legislature fixes the salaries for all members of the major federal organs; it also creates all other permanent federal positions and determines the salaries that shall be paid.

The Federal Assembly has other means of controlling the affairs of the Confederation. In the first place, it is the legislature that approves the annual budget prepared by the Federal Council and all requests for federal loans. During its December session the budget is discussed and voted on, as for any ordinary piece of legislation. Because there is no provision for an extraordinary budget, any unexpected expense must be in the form of a separate demand to the legislature. The budget is not subject to the optional legislative referendum. In the second place, the legislature receives annual operations reports from the other major organs. After examining these reports the legislature can criticize the actions taken and invite the bodies in question to change their conduct. In the case of the Federal Council, the legislature cannot annul decisions already taken; any directives it gives are valid for future action only. The legislature can criticize the manner in which the Federal Tribunal carries out its work but not the judgments rendered. The

---

[2] See above, pp. 63–64.

[3] See Raymond Deonna, *Mémento de l'économie suisse* (Geneva: Les Éditions Radar, 1953), p. 23.

[4] Art. 85, Sec. 4.

Federal Council also prepares an annual financial report which is submitted to the legislature. To insure control over the expenditures of the executive, the legislature has created a special Financial Delegation. This delegation is composed of three members from the Finance Committee of each house and has broad investigative powers.

The legislature plays an essential role in Swiss foreign affairs. It declares war, concludes peace, disposes of the national army, and is generally responsible for taking any other measures necessary for the maintenance of Switzerland's independence and neutrality. The Constitution also gives the legislature the duty of approving all treaties and alliances. As pointed out by Hughes, however, the treaty-making procedure is "remarkably unconstant." Normally the Federal Council negotiates treaties and submits them to the legislature. If the two houses approve, they usually pass an *arrêté* giving the Federal Council the power to ratify. Depending upon the type of treaty, the *arrêté* may be challenged by the people. On the other hand, the legislature may delegate to the Federal Council the power to both negotiate and ratify, or the Council may already have that power as part of the "full powers" granted in the case of a threat of war.[5]

Certain cantonal affairs also come under the jurisdiction of the federal legislature. The Federal Assembly must examine and approve not only all cantonal constitutions and amendments thereto, but also all intercantonal treaties or treaties between cantons and foreign states. The Federal Assembly also has the power to take all measures necessary, including intervention with federal troops, to maintain internal peace. This is a power shared with the Federal Council, and on every occasion requiring federal intervention the Council has been the one to take action. When this has occurred, the Federal Council has convened the legislature to approve its decision.

At one time the legislature also performed important judicial functions. These powers have declined as the jurisdiction of the Federal Tribunal has been increased. It still retains the right to resolve conflicts of jurisdiction between federal authorities, however. In general such conflicts occur between executive and legislative organs and between the Federal Tribunal and the Federal Insurance Tribunal.[6] The Federal Assembly has also reserved judicial authority for itself in certain matters of administrative and public law and in special accusations made by cantons against members of the three major federal organs. For certain offenses, the Federal Assembly retains the right to bring action against any member of a federal organ whom it has

[5] Hughes, *The Federal Constitution of Switzerland*, pp. 93–94.
[6] See Bridel, *Précis . . .* p. 83.

appointed. It may also pardon those convicted by federal judicial authorities and those condemned to death under military law.

Composition

The Swiss federal legislature is made up of two separate bodies, the Council of States and the National Council. As a general rule, they have the same rights and duties; neither is superior to the other. The two bodies meet in joint session only to undertake the following administrative and judicial functions: (1) to elect the Federal Council, the Federal Tribunal, the Federal Insurance Tribunal, the President and Vice-President of the Confederation (the President and Vice-President of the Federal Council), the President and Vice-President of the Federal Tribunal and of the Federal Insurance Tribunal, the Chancellor of the Confederation, and the Commander in Chief of the Army; (2) to exercise the federal pardoning power; and (3) to resolve conflicts of jurisdiction between the major federal organs. When in joint session, the President of the National Council acts as chairman, and the rules of procedure used are primarily those of the National Council. Each member of the two houses has one vote, and decisions are made by a simple majority of those present and voting.

The Council of States

The Council of States is made up of forty-four members, two from each canton and one from each half-canton. The election of representatives to the Council is purely a cantonal matter. In the early days of the 1848 Constitution all members of the Council of State were elected either by cantonal legislatures (unicameral bodies entitled either Cantonal Council or Great Council) or by the *Landsgemeinde* (open meeting of all cantonal voters). The picture has since changed. At present fifteen and a half cantons elect their representatives to the Council of States by direct ballot; four cantons still entrust the election of Councillors to the cantonal legislature (Berne, Fribourg, Neuchâtel, and St. Gallen); and two and a half by the *Landsgemeinde* (Unterwalden, Glarus, and Appenzell-Inner Rhodes).

There is also a certain variation in the terms of the members of the Council of States. In eighteen and a half cantons the term is four years. In Grisons, Glarus, and Obwalden the term is three years. In St. Gallen it is one year.

The only restrictions on elections to the Council of States are contained in Articles 6, 81, and 108 of the Constitution. Article 6 lays down the general rule that all cantonal elections must be "democratic;" Article 81 provides that members of the Council of States may not at the same time be members of the National Council or the Federal Council; and Article 108 makes membership in the Council of States incompatible with membership on the Federal Tribunal. The cantons, however, can add other incompatibilities. In some cantons, for instance, there are limits on the number of members of the cantonal executive who may also serve on the Council of States.

The membership of the Council of States is usually quite stable. Most deputies are re-elected for as long as they wish to serve. The caliber of the individual deputy is also high. Most deputies have made politics a career, rising from communal office to cantonal office. Only those who have proved their worth in cantonal affairs, quite often including membership in the cantonal executives and legislatures, are elected to the Council of States. Most are also well educated. Almost half of the membership of the Council of States in 1960 had been recipients of doctorates.[7]

The National Council

As a result of a constitutional amendment accepted on November 4, 1962, the size of the National Council is fixed at 200 deputies. Each canton and half-canton is guaranteed one representative and the remaining seats are apportioned according to the size of the resident population. As applied to the results of the 1960 census, the cantons now have the following number of deputies: Zurich 35, Berne 33, Vaud 16, Aargau 13, St. Gallen 13, Geneva 10, Lucerne 9, Basle Town 8, Solothurn 7, Ticino 7, Valais 7, Fribourg 6, Thurgau 6, Basle Country 5, Grisons 5, Neuchâtel 5, Schwyz 3, Appenzell-Outer Rhodes 2, Glarus 2, Schaffhausen 2, Zug 2, Appenzell-Inner Rhodes 1, Nidwalden 1, Obwalden 1, and Uri 1.

Prior to the 1962 amendment, the National Council was composed of deputies "chosen in the ratio of one member for each 24,000 souls of the total population." An additional seat was allotted for any fraction over 12,000. Each canton and half-canton was considered as a single election district and was guaranteed one representative. In order to keep the membership in the National Council below two hundred so that it could be accommodated in the Council's chambers, and to keep the membership small enough to work efficiently, the ratio of representatives to population was raised by constitutional amendment on two occasions. In 1931 it was raised from 20,000 to 22,000 and in 1950 from 22,000 to 24,000. As a result of the 1962 amendment, this procedure is no longer necessary.

[7] See Secrétariat de l'Assemblée fédérale, *Membres des Chambres et du Conséil fédéral, 36ᵉᵐᵉ législature* (March, 1960), pp. 16–17.

Election for deputies to the National Council, in contrast to election for the Council of States, is a national matter. The term for National Councillors is fixed at a uniform four years, and the whole body is renewed at each election. In 1931 the term of office was raised from three to four years. General elections are held on the last Sunday in October, and the new legislature meets to organize on the first Monday in December.

"Every lay Swiss citizen entitled to vote is eligible for membership in the National Council."[8] The exclusion of clergy is a leftover from the religious conflicts that preceded the adoption of the 1848 Constitution. In practice this provision affects Catholics more than it does Protestants. A Protestant clergyman would be eligible simply by resigning his office. Since the Catholic clergy supposedly retain their priestly qualities as long as they remain Catholic, they would have to both resign their office and renounce their religion. This provision is also applicable to two other important offices, the Federal Council and the Federal Tribunal.

With this major exception, the conditions for eligibility to the National Council are similar to those for the Council of States. National Councillors may not serve on the Federal Council, the Federal Tribunal, or the Federal Insurance Tribunal. As in the case of the Council of States, the cantons may make other functions incompatible with holding an office for which the Federal Council has appointive power.

As Table 8 demonstrates, the membership of the National Council reflects a diversity of occupational groups. The only really outstanding change in the past fifty years has been in the number of members from the legal profession. In 1916, for instance, there were 78 lawyers out of a total membership of 189, or some 41 per cent. In 1935, lawyers had dropped to 36 out of a total of 187, or 19 per cent. As a result of the 1959 election, the legal profession provided only 10 per cent of the membership of the National Council.[9]

As concerns the ages of the representatives of the people, in 1959 ten members were between 30 and 39 years old, 46 were between 40 and 49, 85 were between 50 and 59, and 55 were 60 years of age or older. At least since 1919, the year of the introduction of proportional representation, there has been a steady shift towards a higher age level. In 1919, 21 per cent of all deputies were in the age bracket 30 to 39, as compared to 5 per cent in 1959. This decline in the number of

[8] Art. 75.
[9] Brooks, *Government and Politics of Switzerland,* p. 100, and Rappard, *The Government of Switzerland,* p. 83.

Table 8

Occupations of Members of the National Council after the Elections of 1959*

Profession	Number
1. Union officials†	34
2. Farmers	24
3. Members of cantonal executive bodies	22
4. Lawyers	21
5. Industrialists, merchants and independent artisans	17
6. Members of municipal councils	17
7. Journalists	16
8. Directors of cooperative societies, private industrial enterprises, etc.**	11
9. Teachers	7
10. Engineers and architects	4
11. Doctors	4
12. Other occupations	19
Total	196

* Bureau Fédéral de Statistique, *Schweizerischen Statistik,* B. 32, Berne, 1961, p. 190.

† Full-time employees of professional organizations such as trade and industrial unions. In French, *fonctionnaires de fédérations,* and in German, *Verbandsfunktionäre.*

** Directeurs de sociétés coopératives et d'enterprises industrielles privées, etc. (Direktoren von Genossenschaften, privaten Industriebetrieben usw.)

younger members has been almost steady, except for a short term rise in the elections of 1935. The group 40 to 49 has remained fairly steady while those 50 to 59 and 60 and over have increased.[10]

Proportional Representation

The 1848 Constitution left the method of election of members of the National Council to the federal legislature. Prior to 1919, the system used was a multi-member district, simple majority system with second ballot. First the cantons were assigned the number of seats to which their size entitled them. Except for the restrictions that each canton would have at least one deputy and that election districts could not cut across cantonal borders, the federal legislature was free to determine the size of the districts and the number of deputies to be elected in each. In 1910, for example, there were two eight-member

[10] Bureau Fédéral de Statistique, *Schweizerischen Statistik,* B. 32, Berne, 1961, p. 189.

districts, five seven-member districts, three six-member districts, six five-member districts, ten four-member districts, ten three-member districts, seven two-member districts, and six one-member districts. In every district, each voter was entitled to vote for as many candidates as there were seats to be filled. On the first ballot an absolute majority was essential for election. For seats not thus filled on the first ballot, a supplementary election was held two or three weeks later, at which time a simple plurality was sufficient for election.[11]

In 1919 a system of proportional representation was introduced for the election of National Council members. As with many other national political institutions, it was adopted after successful usage on a cantonal basis. Party strife which had led to two federal interventions was eliminated in Ticino with the introduction of proportional representation in 1892. Neuchâtel and Zug followed in 1894, Solothurn in 1895, Basle Town in 1905, Schwyz in 1907, Lucerne in 1909, St. Gallen in 1911, and Zurich in 1916. The first initiative to introduce proportional representation for the election of members of the National Council was rejected in 1900. A second initiative was defeated in 1910. Although favored by a majority of the cantons it did not receive a majority of the popular vote. Proportional representation was finally adopted in 1918, and used for the first time in the 1919 elections.

Because the initiative also designated the canton as the election district, proportional representation in Switzerland has been important only in the cantons that send more than one candidate to the National Council.

The method of proportional representation adopted was the flexible list system. The making of party lists is a cantonal matter. To become eligible a party must present a list of its candidates to the cantonal authorities, with fifteen signatures of qualified electors, within a prescribed time limit before the election. In the 1959 elections, for instance, the limit was 34 days. The lists may contain fewer names than the number of seats assigned to the canton, but in no case more. If his name appears on more than one list, the candidate must, within thirty days preceding the election, choose the party on whose list he wishes to be presented. After scrutiny by the cantonal authorities for conformance to law, the lists are given to the Federal Council. The federal law permits official lists to be printed by either the canton or the political parties; the decision is up to the cantonal authorities. The voters receive the lists at the polling places on election day.

The voter is given as many votes as there are seats to be filled. He

[11] Brooks, pp. 73–75.

may cast one of the party ballots as it stands; he may eliminate some names with the option of replacing them with names from other lists (*panachage*); or he may cast his votes by composing his own list of candidates on an official non-partisan blank ballot.[12] On no individual ballot may the number of votes cast exceed the number of seats to be filled, and in all cantons where there are two seats or more in contest only names that appear on the official lists may be used. (The voter also may vote twice for one or more candidates.)[13] Although this latter provision effectively eliminates write-in candidates, the small number of electors required to create an official list renders it sufficiently easy for any serious candidate to place his name before the public. It goes without saying that such a procedure does not have the effect of limiting the number of parties.

After the ballots have been cast, the problem arises of determining first the number of seats each party has won and second which of the party's candidates have been elected. The total of all the party votes is first divided by the number of seats to be filled plus one.[14] The result is the "provisional quotient." The provisional quotient is used to determine how many seats each party receives.

If, as often is the case, there remain unapportioned seats after the quotient is applied, further assessments are made. In the second and

[12] The Swiss voter understands his electoral system sufficiently to make use of the freedom of choice that it offers him. In the 1955 elections, only 60.6 per cent of the voters cast unaltered party ballots (70.8 per cent in 1935). Of the remainder, *panachage* accounted for 14.5 per cent and non-partisan ballots for another 2.7 per cent. The use of straight party ballots depends to a large extent on the party in question. Of the major parties, the Socialists seem to have more discipline in these matters. In 1955 the number of straight party ballots cast by Socialists amounted to 74 per cent, by the Catholic Conservatives 54.3 per cent, and by the Radicals 53.0 per cent. There is also a great diversity among cantons. In Valais, with seven seats to be filled, only one third of the voters in 1955 used straight party ballots while in Geneva with eight seats to be filled, 83.7 per cent used straight ballots. See, Bureau fédéral de statistique, *Élections au Conseil National, 1955,* Berne, 1958, pp. 61–91. The casting of blank ballots in Switzerland is minimal. In 1955, blank ballots accounted for only 1.7 per cent of those cast. As would be expected, the percentage of such ballots was high in the cantons with compulsory voting. In St. Gallen, there were 2,234 blank ballots out of a total of 68,900; in Aargau, 2,342 out of 79,494; and in Thurgau, 764 out of 32,296. *Ibid.,* pp. 60 & 85.

[13] Bridel, p. 61. The party too may list a name twice on its official ballot.

[14] It should be noted that the total party votes may differ from the total votes cast for candidates. Take, for example, an election in which there are five seats to be filled on the National Council. If an elector should eliminate one of the five names on an official ballot without substituting another or should substitute an unauthorized one, the party still would receive five votes.

subsequent assessments, the total of each party's vote is divided by the number of seats already gained, plus one. The first remaining seat is given to the party with the highest remainder. The process is continued until all the seats have been allotted. The following example from Bridel should make the process clear.

In the canton of Solothurn there were seven seats to be filled and five parties in the running. The total party vote was 270,322. By dividing the total party vote by eight (seven plus one) the quotient turned out to be 33,791. The quotient was applied to each party's vote with the following results:

First Round

Party	Vote	Quotient	Seats Assigned
1. Radical	99,559	33,791	2
2. Socialists	85,348	33,791	2
3. Peasants	8,188	33,791	0
4. Catholics	66,979	33,791	1
5. Independents	10,248	33,791	0

The party to which the first of the two remaining seats was allotted was determined by dividing the party votes by the number of seats each obtained in the first round, plus one:

1. Radicals $\quad$ $99,559 \div 3 \ (2+1) = 33,186\frac{1}{3}$
2. Socialists $\quad$ $85,348 \div 3 \ (2+1) = 28,449\frac{1}{3}$
3. Peasants $\quad$ $8,188 \div 1 \ (0+1) = \ 8,188$
4. Catholics $\quad$ $66,979 \div 2 \ (1+1) = 33,489\frac{1}{2}$ (seat assigned)
5. Independents $\quad$ $10,248 \div 1 \ (0+1) = 10,248$

In this case the last round would occur when this process is repeated. The only difference is that the Catholic vote would be divided by 3 (1 from the first round, 1 from the second round, plus 1). The results for the Catholics would be $22,326\frac{1}{3}$. Thus, the remaining seat would be allotted to the Radicals who have the highest remainder $(33,186\frac{1}{3})$. The final results would be: Radicals, 3 seats; Socialists, 2 seats; Catholics, 2 seats.[15]

The election of candidates within each party depends upon their individual votes. If a seat on the National Council should fall vacant between elections, it is given to the candidate of the same party who had the most votes among those not elected.[16]

[15] Bridel, pp. 69–70.

[16] If announced when party lists are submitted, the law permits alliances between parties. For the manner in which seats are distributed between allied parties, see Bridel, p. 71.

Organization

According to the Constitution, the two chambers meet only once a year in ordinary session. In actual fact, the Federal Assembly meets four times a year, in March, June, September, and December. A legal fiction is employed to circumvent the Constitution — the meeting in December is designated as the first part of the ordinary session and the meeting in June as the second part. The meeting in March is called a continuation of the first part of the ordinary session and the meeting in September a continuation of the second part. As a result of this fiction, there is no need to renew the internal organization of the two houses. The length of the meetings depends upon the number of matters to be discussed, but usually is from two to three weeks. The two legislative houses must always be in session at the same time, but the hours and the length of the work week need not coincide. Most meetings start at eight in the morning, and sessions are held every day except Saturday and Sunday (and Monday for the Council of States).

Extraordinary sessions may be called on the demand of the Federal Council, of a quarter of the members of the National Council, or of five cantons. (The Council of States does not have a say in the calling of an extraordinary session.) The usual procedure is for the Federal Council to call for extraordinary sessions when it feels that the pressure of business so demands or in the case of an emergency situation such as external danger. The cantons have never exercised their right, and the National Council on only one occasion in 1891.[17]

Preparation for work in the Swiss legislature is a fairly simple matter. A few weeks before the first session of the National Council in December, the oldest member (*doyen d'âge*) forms a temporary bureau to prepare for the opening of the session and to appoint a temporary credentials committee. At the first meeting, presided over by the *doyen,* the Council receives a report of this committee. As soon as the National Council, all present voting, verifies the election of an absolute majority, the Council is considered constituted. Because the Council of States is considered to be a continuing organ, it does not have recourse to temporary bodies, but uses the organization carried over from the preceding session. Further, since elections to the Council of States is a cantonal matter, its only task in the matter of credentials is to accept communications from the cantons concerning election of members.

Each of the two houses elects a President and Vice-President, and determines its own internal organization. The rules of both houses

[17] Hughes, p. 98.

provide for a permanent bureau made up of the President, Vice-President, and a small group of tellers. In keeping with the Swiss tradition of doing everything possible to eliminate the likelihood of any one person or any one canton gaining too much power, the same man may not be elected to the Presidency or Vice-Presidency for two successive ordinary sessions. After a year in office, however, the Vice-President may be elected to succeed the President.

Because both houses are small, the duties of the presiding officers are minimal. Delegates usually may talk as long and as often as they wish. While the presidents have the usual powers of recognition, speeches usually are given in the order in which a request is made. If some one should abuse his privilege of free speech, the President may warn the deputy, call him to order, or, in the case of extreme situations, take away his right to speak. Deputies may speak in any one of the three official languages — French, German, or Italian. The presidents cast the deciding votes in cases of ties.

The Swiss Constitution provides that the Councils may conduct business only when an absolute majority is present. In the case of the Council of States the quorum is 23 (one more than half the 44 members), and in the National Council it is 101 (one more than half the 200 members). Deputies are obliged to attend all meetings; their per diem is withheld if they are absent. This provision does not, of course, guarantee the constant presence of all of the members of the legislature in the chambers. The individual deputies may be out telephoning, talking to constituents, or engaging in any of the other activities that occupy the time of legislators around the world. However, since the members do not have personal offices, as do United States Congressmen, and since the Swiss legislative chambers are comfortable, the attendance for routine legislative work is usually more impressive than that of some other legislatures.

All decisions are made by a majority of those voting with the exception of the approval of "urgent" *arrêtés* which, being exempt from the legislative referendum, require the approval of a majority of all the members of the two houses. Decisions are made by voice vote on all occasions other than the election of federal officials; in the latter, the secret ballot is utilized. Each house has its rules of procedure for making meetings secret, but almost all meetings are open to the public. All important debates are reported in the official *Bulletin sténographique*.

As is customary with most parliamentary bodies, the Swiss parliament has recourse to committees for the expedition of business. The size of the committee depends upon the importance of the matters under its authority, but its composition must provide for an equitable representation of political parties and language groups. Committees are permanent or *ad hoc* as the needs of the chamber dictate. The largest permanent committee in the 1960 session was the National Council Committee on Customs — twenty-nine members — and the smallest was the Council of States Committee on Pardons — four members. In the 1960 session the National Council had twelve permanent committees and the Council of States ten.[18]

Swiss deputies do not receive a salary for service in the Federal Assembly. National Councillors receive a per diem paid from the national treasury for each day the legislature is in session. Councillors of State receive a per diem from their cantons. A per diem and a travel allowance is given to both by the national treasury when attending meetings of committees between legislative sessions. In addition, deputies are exempt from military service during tenure in office and need not pay the military exemption tax.

There are certain rules and regulations imposed on all Swiss deputies to ensure that they will carry out their functions properly. Article 91 of the Constitution, for instance, provides that "members of the two Councils shall vote without instructions." Instructions from any source are theoretically included: political parties, cantons, or interest groups. In voting, deputies must use their own consciences as their guides.

Deputies are also recipients of certain immunities. All are guaranteed by federal law the freedom of speech and debate; they cannot be held responsible except to their own chamber. Neither the Confederation nor the deputies can be held responsible for the results of laws passed. In judicial proceedings, a deputy has immunity during the session of the legislature unless that immunity is withdrawn by his own Council. If the proceedings have been begun before the opening of a session, a judgment may be withheld until the session has ended. A deputy can be arrested for the commission of a serious crime while parliament is in session, but cannot be held unless, with the agreement of his Council, the authorities request the withdrawal of immunity within twenty-four hours of the arrest.

[18] *Membres des Chambres et du Conseil fédéral,* p. 28. The two permanent committees of the National Council which did not have their counterpart in the Council of States were the Credentials Committee and the Committee on the Post, Telegraph and Telephone Administration. Both Councils had these permanent committees: (1) Finances; (2) Administration (*Commission de gestion*); (3) Alcohol; (4) Petitions; (5) Pardons; (6) Railway Concessions; (7) Federal Railways; (8) Customs; (9) Foreign Affairs; and (10) Military Affairs.

Lawmaking Procedure

The Swiss Constitution gives the right to introduce a bill to both the National Council and the Council of States, to each member of the two houses, to each canton and half-canton, and to the Federal Council. In practice, the Federal Council has taken upon itself the responsibility for introducing bills into the Swiss federal legislature.

Most bills not only are introduced by the Federal Council, but also stem from its initiative. When the Council feels that a piece of legislation is necessary for the proper functioning of government, or when it decides that there is a popular desire for a new law, it proceeds to draft a bill with the help of its professional staff. The draft, along with a report setting forth the Council's views on the matter, is presented to the two houses for consideration. This is usually the procedure.

If in the opinion of the Federal Assembly other legislation is needed, it does not introduce it itself, but requests the Council to act through procedures known as the "motion" and the "postulate." A motion is a command to the Council to act. It must receive the agreement of both houses. The postulate is of lesser gravity, but leads toward the same objective. Rather than commanding the Federal Council to submit a draft law, the postulate merely "invites" the Federal Council to act. The postulate stems from only one house of the legislature, rather than both as is the case with a motion. Upon receipt of a motion or postulate, the Federal Council proceeds to draft a bill along the lines suggested. The draft bill and the Council's report are presented to the Assembly. The Council may include also a recommendation to the Assembly to reject the bill. Although the Council usually gives serious consideration to postulates and motions, it does not necessarily comply. Motions "are deemed to lapse when the signatories cease to be members of the Council, or if the motion is not discussed at all within two years, or is not answered by the Federal Council within four years."[19] Postulates have an even shorter life span if not taken up by the Federal Council.[20]

Neither house has priority on the discussion of a bill. Consequently, at the first session of the legislature the Federal Council submits its bills and messages to the presidents of both the National Council and the Council of States. The presidents decide between themselves which house will be the first to discuss each piece of business. Unless the Federal Council has designated a bill as especially urgent, the division of business must be sanctioned by each house. If it has been so desig-

[19] Hughes, p. 149.
[20] Hughes, p. 150.

nated, the decision of the two presidents is binding. Should it happen that the two houses are unable to agree on the matter of priority on regular business, this is decided by the casting of lots.

Ordinarily the bills allotted the two Councils are sent immediately to the appropriate committee. In contrast to usual American practice, Swiss legislative committees carry on the bulk of their work in the interim between legislative sessions. They do not confine their meetings to the capital city, but convene in various cities in Switzerland at their pleasure. This practice is undoubtedly rewarding for committee members, and at the same time it tends to give the cities and cantons in which they meet a sense of participation in national affairs. The committees receive the secretarial assistance of the Federal Chancellery and may call upon federal officials or even members of the Federal Council for questioning. Although the committees seldom change the sense of the draft law, suggestions for amendment often are made. Minority reports frequently accompany the majority reports of the committee to its Council.

There are three major stages in the discussion of proposed legislation in each house. After receiving the report of its committee, the Council with priority first debates "entering upon the matter." If this is agreed upon, the Council then proceeds to an article-by-article debate. After this debate, the bill is voted upon as a whole. If approved, the bill is then sent to the other house where the procedure is repeated. In exceptional cases, and in the event the draft bill is capable of being broken up logically, each house simultaneously may take different sections of the same bill for debate. As soon as each section is approved by one house, it is sent immediately to the other for consideration.

The Law on the Relations Between Councils of 1902, as amended in 1939, sets forth the procedure to be followed in the case of disagreement between the two houses. If the second house disagrees with the decisions of the first, it sends the bill back for another deliberation. Only the points of difference are discussed, unless the changes are of such a nature as to necessitate a debate on the bill as a whole. This procedure continues until agreement is reached, or until the two bodies agree to disagree. In that event, the points of difference are submitted to a joint conference committee presided over by a member of the house which had the original priority in the matter. The proposals of this committee for eliminating the differences are submitted first to the house that had original priority. If the conference committee cannot reach an acceptable alternative, or if their proposals are refused, the bill in question is considered rejected.

When a bill has been passed in identical form by both houses, the

Federal Chancellery prepares an official text which is signed by the presidents and secretaries of both Councils. The text is then submitted to the Federal Council for publication and execution. Laws come into effect, unless challenged by referendum, on the date fixed in the original bill or, if no date is mentioned, within five days after publication.

The Decline of Legislative Supremacy

On the one hand, it cannot be said in truth that there is any real discontent among the Swiss over the operation of their federal legislature. It provides a national forum for the expression of differing points of view, it works quietly and without undue haste, and its cost is not excessive. Despite the anxiety of the founding fathers, its bicameral nature did not create any great problems. The two houses have managed to work together without excessive friction. In fact, seldom does one house seriously attempt to overthrow the decisions of the other on matters of national importance. Further, the caliber of men who serve in the Assembly is uniformly high and election to one of the two Councils is still a great honor.

On the other hand, it cannot be denied that the Swiss parliament as a body does not enjoy the prestige that the framers of the Constitution of 1848 thought it should have. Many reasons are given for this phenomenon, the most important of which seem to be: (1) the institutions of direct democracy and the use to which they are put, and (2) the rise in importance of the Swiss federal executive. As concerns direct democracy, the Swiss legislature has to work with the knowledge that almost any fundamental law that it passes may be subject to a legislative referendum. Such a situation cannot help but have a tendency to create an atmosphere of doubt or indecision, if not a feeling of helplessness. As we have seen, the Swiss electorate is not adverse to using its weapon of direct democracy. It is felt by many that it has actually led to a reluctance on the part of the Assembly to take the lead in creating new legislation, preferring to await the leadership of the Federal Council or the threat of a constitutional initiative. Consequently, the legislature has been reduced, to a certain extent, to the position of an advisory body with the electorate exercising the real decision-making power. If a system of legislative initiative should also be adopted, as is being suggested, there is little doubt that the prestige of the legislature would be even further lowered.

The position of importance that the Federal Council has created for itself, despite the obvious intent of the Constitution to make the legislature supreme, will become more evident as we examine this body in detail in the next chapter. It will suffice at this point to conclude that the Swiss federal legislature is no longer the body envisioned by the framers of the Constitutions of 1848 and 1874, having abandoned many of its functions to the federal executive and to the people themselves.

✛ 6 ✛

The Federal Council

The unique institution of this unique little country is without doubt the Federal Council, the Swiss federal executive. Composed of seven men elected by the Federal Assembly, the Federal Council combines what the Swiss consider the best qualities of the democratic presidential and cabinet systems. In its operation it also exemplifies the qualities the Swiss consider essential at any level of government — stability, anonymity, and efficiency.

In their examination of American institutions for possible adoption in the new governmental system, the Swiss in 1848 took a long look at the office of the American chief executive. The possibility of having a strong executive, or at least a single individual to represent the state in international affairs, was recognized, debated, and finally rejected. The experience of various neighbors on the European continent was too fresh and repellent. The committee that drafted the 1848 Constitution noted in its report that the Swiss might see in the creation of a strong executive "evidence of a monarchial or dictatorial tendency." Further, "our democratic feeling revolts against any exclusive personal pre-eminence."[1]

Having rejected the American model, and finding nothing pertinent in the experience of other states, the framers of the 1848 Constitution turned to local practice. Many Swiss cantons had, for a long time past, found that cantonal affairs could be managed without difficulty by a small group of individuals elected by cantonal parliaments. Despite the wider range of activities that would exist on a national scale, and the heavier load of responsibilities that would be expected, the framers decided to emulate the cantons. And, as we shall see, the decision was a good one.

[1] See Rappard, *The Government of Switzerland*, p. 76.

Consequently, the Swiss Federal Constitution entrusts the "supreme directing and executive power in the Confederation" to a Federal Council composed of seven members.[2] These seven men, elected every four years by the Swiss parliament, have successfully directed the affairs of state since 1848 despite a steadily increasing work load and both internal and external crises.

Before proceeding to a more detailed analysis of the powers and functions of this body, it should be noted that despite superficial similarities the Federal Council is no more comparable to the cabinet system of government than it is to the American executive. All seven men are elected individually by the legislature. Being elected for a fixed term of office, Federal Councillors are not "responsible" to the parliament for their actions. That is to say, they are not impelled to resign if their policies are rejected by the legislature. The legislature can refuse to elect a Councillor in whom they have lost confidence — it has occurred twice since 1848 — but a Federal Councillor has never been forced to resign.

Composition

The legal qualifications for election to the Federal Council are few. Any Swiss citizen eligible for election to the National Council may be elected to the Federal Council. Not more than one member, however, can be elected from the same canton. A federal law dating from 1914 adds one other provision: "Persons related by blood or marriage without limit in the direct line and up to and including the fourth degree in the collateral line, husbands who have married sisters, and also persons connected by adoption, may not at the same time be members of the Federal Council."[3]

The legal qualifications are supplemented by several rigidly obeyed customs. The first of these is that the membership of the Federal Council will reflect the geographical power concentrations in the federation. Custom prescribes that Berne and Zurich, the two cantons with the largest population and the traditional leaders in federal politics, shall always be represented. The second, to assure that the minority language groups will be represented, dictates that not more than five of the seven Federal Councillors may come from the German-speaking cantons. In practice this is interpreted by electing a member from Vaud, the largest of the French cantons, and one other from either another French-speaking canton or the Italian-speaking Ticino. The third qualification, one that has had some difficulty in being completely accepted but that probably has become fixed as a result of the

[2] Art. 95.
[3] Brooks, *Government and Politics of Switzerland,* pp. 104–105.

1959 elections, decrees that the composition of the Federal Council reflect as closely as possible the power of all the major political parties.

Two additional practices tend to limit the choice of candidates for the Federal Council. It is almost an invariable practice to select persons who have had considerable experience in public affairs. This usually means that candidates are chosen from among members of the National Council or Council of States, although individuals who have served on the more important cantonal bodies are not ineligible.

With two exceptions, once in 1854 and once in 1872, the Swiss legislature has re-elected Federal Councillors as long as they wished to serve. Thus most Councillors serve at least two or three terms. In some cases service extended twenty-five to thirty years. This system consequently provides for great stability in the direction of federal affairs. Since the Councillors have also served in the federal legislature and in high cantonal offices previously, the system provides a large degree of administrative skill and political acumen in the members of the Federal Council.

There is an additional qualification for election to the Federal Council, one that is a little difficult for an American to explain and perhaps to understand, but a real one nevertheless. No matter how well qualified on other accounts, no one can expect to be elected to the Federal Council unless he reflects the virtue which, above all others, the Swiss demand of those who hold public office — modesty. In his previous cantonal and national service, he must have left an image of a person dedicated to his work without thought of personal recognition. The office must seek the candidate, not the candidate the office. While this is true for most important offices, it is especially true for the Federal Council. The election of 1959 was a good example. At that time the Federal Assembly refused to accept a Socialist candidate for one of the two seats allotted to the Socialists, despite the fact that the candidate was at the same time the President of the Swiss Socialist party and had many years of service on both the cantonal and federal levels. This came about because he had helped establish the Swiss Communist party in his early years, and he was an older man — the Assembly was looking for youth. But the major determining factor was undoubtedly the fact that he was an excellent orator and in general gave a too obvious impression of a man who "wanted the job." As several observers of the election stated to the author, he was a little too *flamboyant.*[4]

---

[4] The Swiss government did not completely lose the services of M. Walter Bringolf, the man in question, however. In December, 1960, the National Council chose him as its new Vice-President and in December, 1961, he became its President.

Elections to the Federal Council take place every four years, a few weeks after the new National Council is formed, usually the second or third week in December. Each of the seven seats is filled individually. Selection begins from among those members who have signified that they wish to remain in office, and priority is given to the individual with the longest service within that group. Next the vacant seats are filled. If there is more than one, precedence is accorded to the vacancy created by the retired Councillor with the longest tenure. If two or more of the retired Councillors had the same length of service, the seat of the oldest one is filled first. A majority of the votes cast is sufficient for election. The procedure is as follows. Each member of the Federal Assembly writes the name of the man of his choice on a blank ballot. The ballot is placed in an urn that is passed from member to member. If no man receives a majority on the first ballot, which is usually the case, another vote is held. On the third ballot nominations are closed and the name with the fewest number of votes is dropped. The whole procedure is repeated until some candidate receives a clear majority. Before 1900 repeated balloting was often required before new members of the Council were elected, but since that time three consecutive ballots rarely have been necessary.

In view of the custom that any Councillor who signifies that he wishes to remain in office is automatically re-elected, elections usually are a mere formality with only one seat being filled by a new member at any one time. The choice of an appropriate candidate is actually made by the political party whose turn it is, after consultation with the other major parties. Nevertheless, after receiving the necessary majority, the successful candidate is called before the Assembly to state whether or not he accepts his election.

Once elected, a Federal Councillor can hold no positions, either public or private, that could in any way interfere with his duties. If he was a member of the National Council or the Council of States he immediately loses that position upon election to the new post. Furthermore, during office he may not occupy "any official position either in the service of the confederation or of a canton, nor may he engage in any other calling or profession."[5] While this provision insures that members of the Federal Council will have no conflicting responsibilities, in the past it has also meant that they were not able to live in any form of luxury unless they had an independent source of income. In 1848 the compensation for a Federal Councillor was fixed at a little over $1,000 a year (5,000 Swiss francs). Over the years the salary has been slowly augmented. In 1959 the pay of a Councillor was raised to about

[5] Art. 97.

$15,000 (65,000 Swiss francs), certainly an improvement, but still modest remuneration for one of the most important posts in his nation. The President receives in addition an expense allowance of 5,000 francs. After five years in office, Federal Councillors are eligible for a pension calculated on the basis of age and years of service.

In general Federal Councillors receive the same immunities as members of the Federal Assembly. All are exempt from military service during their terms of office. They cannot be subjects of criminal proceedings while in office unless the Federal Council itself lifts the immunity. However, if the Federal Council should refuse, the case could be taken to the Federal Assembly. In any case, if immunity is lifted, Federal Councillors can be tried only by the Federal Tribunal.

Each Federal Councillor must live in Berne during his term of office, and Berne alone can levy a tax on the salary he receives from the Confederation. On the other hand, the Councillor retains his home canton as the canton in which he exercises his civil and political rights.

The Federal Council acts as a collegiate body; thus decisions always come from the body as a whole. Since the deliberations of the Federal Council are secret, and former members of the Federal Council are reluctant to recount their experiences, it is difficult to state definitely how much diversity of opinion ordinarily exists. It seems quite evident, however, that most routine decisions are made by a Councillor competent in the matter and with later perfunctory ratification by the group as a whole.

The few legal rules regulating the conduct of business of the Federal Council do not tend to negate the above conclusion. The Council must meet at least once a week, and four members constitute a quorum. Decisions are taken on a majority basis, but all the decisions must be supported by at least three members.

The President of the Confederation

Once a year the Federal Assembly elects a member of the Federal Council to serve as President of the Confederation and a second to serve as Vice-President. The Constitution prohibits the re-election of the President or Vice-President for two years in succession. By custom, the Vice-President succeeds the President, and the two offices are rotated among the members of the Federal Council. Usually the new members of the Council must await the re-election of the older members before taking their turns as President and Vice-President.

The powers of the President of the Confederation are nominal. His most important functions are chairing the Federal Council and acting as the titular head of state at home and abroad. The President also has certain very limited emergency powers — in certain cases he may be empowered to act in the name of the Council with the understanding that whatever he does must be submitted later to the Council for its approval — he exercises general supervisory power over the work of the Council, and he is responsible for the Federal Chancellery. As the Swiss say, the President of the Confederation is only "the first among equals."

Under the 1849 law the President of the Confederation also held the post of head of the Federal Political (Foreign) Department. Inasmuch as the Presidency was rotated, the head of the Political Department also changed every year. While such an arrangement had the advantage that members of the Council became acquainted with the work of all federal departments, it did not necessarily provide for continuity in the direction of foreign affairs. After two trial periods, 1887–1894 and 1915–1917, the Presidency was dissociated from the Political Department. At present a Federal Councillor usually remains in charge of the Department to which he was first appointed.

Legislative Responsibilities

It is in the legislative process where the true authority of the Federal Council makes itself known. Section 4 of Article 102 of the Swiss Constitution reads: "It [the Federal Council] submits drafts of laws and *arrêtés* to the Federal Assembly and makes a preliminary report upon proposals submitted to it by the Councils or the Cantons." On the basis of this provision alone, the Federal Council has become the director of the Swiss legislative process.

As mentioned in the preceding chapter, the bulk of all new legislation is originated by the Federal Council. Even in cases where the legislative councils are of the opinion that the Federal Council has failed to anticipate the need for a law, the councils themselves do not usually initiate legislation but instead make a formal request to the Federal Council to do so. With the help of its expert staff, the Federal Council drafts the bill and presents it to the Federal Assembly, along with a well-reasoned report presenting the purpose of the proposed legislation and giving the reasons why it should or should not be enacted. Even in the cases where the Assembly has requested the Federal Council to draft a piece of legislation, it usually does not enact the draft law when the Council's report is unfavorable.

The Federal Council's task does not end with the submission of draft bills. As a general rule, a Federal Councillor is assigned to guide the bill all the way through the legislative process. He meets with the committee to which the bill has been delivered. It is examined in his presence, and he gives his advice and comments as the committee proceeds with its work. As stated by Professor Rappard: "It is not necessary to have attended many such meetings to understand why the principal actors are rarely the legislative members."[6] When the bill comes to the floor of one of the legislative houses, the Federal Councillor is there to introduce the measure, to explain its meanings, to defend it if necessary, and in general to act as its shepherd before the legislative wolves. Again in the words of Professor Rappard, "one is forced to admit that the most responsible and influential work is that not of the so-called legislature, but of the executive."[7] The Federal Council sees to the printing of all bills passed by the legislature and often fixes the date of entry into force of new legislation, in cases where the Assembly fails to do so.

Despite its prerogatives, however, the Federal Council is not free from accountability to the legislature. Deputies of both the National Council and the Council of States are given the right of "interpellation." An interpellation is a request for an explanation addressed to the Federal Council in writing. It must be supported by ten deputies in the National Council or three in the Council of States. The deputy who initiates an interpellation is given the opportunity to develop his arguments on the floor. A member of the Federal Council may reply immediately or at a later session. After the reply has been made, the deputy who initiated the interpellation is given the opportunity only to declare himself satisfied or not with the Federal Councillor's reply. Unless the deputy's chamber should so decide, which is rarely the case, neither debate nor vote takes place. If the legislator in question is unsatisfied, his only alternative is to have recourse to a motion or postulate.

In the National Council, the interpellation is often replaced by the written question. In this case the question for which a reply is desired is handed in writing to the President of the National Council who passes it on to the Federal Council. As in the case of an interpellation, the Federal Council is supposed to reply before the end of the next regularly scheduled session. In principle, however, neither the question nor the reply is discussed on the floor. Since 1946, the National Council has also made use of a "question hour," based on the British example, in which members of the lower house may question members of the Federal Council directly on any subject concerning the federal administration. In the question hour at the beginning of the September, 1960, session, for example, the Federal Council replied to several

[6] Rappard, p. 83.
[7] *Ibid.*, p. 84.

dozen questions including one requesting the Federal Council to investigate the possibilities of recruiting workers for Swiss industries from Spain and Greece. One asked whether it would be feasible to install more mechanical warning systems at railroad crossings, and one asked whether the Federal Bank should not use new "anti-germ" paper for Swiss bank notes.

Executive Responsibilities

Article 95 of the Swiss Constitution designates the Federal Council as "the supreme directing and executive authority of the Confederation." As the chief executive of Switzerland, the Federal Council is entrusted with most of the duties that its counterpart has in other governments, although much of its responsibility is shared with other organs of the Swiss government.

In the first place, the Federal Council is responsible for the conduct of Swiss foreign affairs. The Federal Council, through the member who is President of the Confederation, is the official spokesman for the Swiss nation. This includes receiving foreign ambassadors and ministers and appointing Swiss ambassadors and ministers to foreign countries. The Federal Council also negotiates treaties and ratifies them after approval of the legislature.

The Federal Council is also charged with the preservation of both the internal and external security of Switzerland. In peacetime these duties include the organization of the Swiss military forces. The details of this authority will be discussed in a later chapter. In case of emergency, and when the Federal Assembly is not in session, the Federal Council can use Swiss troops as it sees fit to put down internal disturbances or to defend Swiss frontiers. As mentioned earlier, if more than two thousand men are called up, or if they are kept mobilized for more than three weeks, the Federal Council must call an emergency meeting of the General Assembly to approve its actions.

The execution of the decisions of the legislature is the third major area of Federal Council responsibility. While the Council is relieved of many duties in this sphere, because the execution of many federal laws is entrusted to the cantons, it retains general supervisory powers. The Federal Council supervises the manner in which the cantons enforce federal laws, *arrêtés,* and federal judicial decisions. It is also entrusted with the execution and enforcement of arbitral decisions dealing with disputes between cantons, and the examination and approval of certain types of cantonal laws and ordinances. If a canton should fail to carry out its obligations, or refuse suggestions by the Federal Council, the Council can carry the matter to the courts or if necessary to the General Assembly. As an ultimate weapon, it can always use its power to call out federal troops. It has charge of drawing up the federal budget and the ofttimes odious task of defending it before the federal legislature.

The Ordinance Power

The increasingly complex nature of governmental activities has resulted in the delegation by the Federal Assembly to the Federal Council of a great deal of discretion in the administration of federal law. Rather than spell out the details of the execution of laws, which in many cases the legislators are not competent to do, the General Assembly will state the intent of the law in general terms and grant the Federal Council the power to fix the details of application and to issue the necessary rules and regulations. The rules and regulations subsequently issued by the Federal Council have the force of law and can be upheld in courts. They have an additional advantage in Switzerland in that they cannot be subject to the legislative referendum as are many legislative laws and *arrêtés*. There has been a steady increase in the number of such ordinances, even in normal times. In the period 1920 to 1929, for instance, it has been estimated that twice as many ordinances were issued from the executive branch of the government as laws and *arrêtés* promulgated by the federal legislature.[8]

In times of emergency, the ordinance power practically replaces normal legislation. It has become a custom at such times for the Federal Assembly to grant the Federal Council "full powers" to issue any ordinances it sees fit for the protection of Switzerland's neutrality and economic stability. Such powers were granted in 1848, 1853, 1859, and 1870, but the Federal Council did not find it necessary to use them. They were granted again in 1914 and used extensively until the grant was withdrawn by the legislature in 1919. Extraordinary economic power was granted to the Federal Council in 1930 and used until replaced by the "full powers" of 1939.

One of the most sweeping grants of power to any democratic executive whose country was not actually engaged in war was given in 1939 to the Federal Council. It was passed in the form of an urgent federal *arrêté*, not subject to the legislative referendum, only one day after being requested by the Federal Council. The two most important sections of the *arrêté* read as follows:

[8] See Deonna, *Mémento de l'économie suisse*, p. 23. The term *arrêté*, among others, is used to describe rules or ordinances issued by the Federal Council. A Federal Council *arrêté* should not be confused with one issued by the legislature.

Article 3. The Federal Assembly grants to the Federal Council the power and the duty to take the measures necessary to maintain the security, independence, and neutrality of Switzerland, to safeguard the credit and economic interests of the country, and to secure its supply of food.

Article 4. The credits necessary for this purpose are granted to the Federal Council. In addition, the power is granted to the Federal Council to contract the necessary loans.[9]

Some of the specific actions taken by the Federal Council under this grant of powers will be discussed in the chapter dealing with Swiss domestic policies. At this point it will suffice to observe that while it was in effect, the Federal Council took upon itself many powers normally belonging to the Federal Assembly and to the cantonal legislatures.

In 1945 the Federal Assembly passed another *arrêté* which called upon the Federal Council to rescind all measures taken under its grant of full powers except those that the Council felt were still necessary. Finally, in 1950, the legislature decreed that all acts passed under the grant should cease to be in force at the end of 1952 unless prolonged by normal legislative procedure.[10]

Administration

The executive branch of the Swiss federal government is organized under seven administrative departments. Each member of the Federal Council is the head of one department and the substitute head of one other. The Federal Council decides itself how the functions are to be distributed. In 1963 the departments and assignments of the Federal Councillors were as follows:

Department	Head	Substitute Head
Political	Wahlen	Chaudet
Interior	Tschudi	von Moos
Justice and Police	von Moos	Bonvin
Military	Chaudet	Spühler
Finance and Customs	Bonvin	Tschudi
Public Economy	Schaffner	Wahlen
Posts and Railways	Spühler	Schaffner

The interior organization of each of the departments is established by federal law. Since there are only seven Federal Councillors, and

[9] From the translation in Hughes, *The Federal Constitution of Switzerland,* pp. 170–171.
[10] See Hughes, p. 168.

thus only seven departments, it is necessary to keep shuffling the specific duties of the departments as new tasks are given the federal government, in order to maintain an equitable distribution of functions.

In general the titles of most of the departments are self-explanatory. Each one, however, exercises some functions that one would not normally consider associated with its duties. The Political Department, for example, carries out the functions equivalent to those of the State Department in the United States or the Ministry of Foreign Affairs in the United Kingdom. In addition, it has a division for relations with the numerous international oganizations that have their headquarters in Switzerland, and a division of press and information. In its wide range of duties, the Department of the Interior is also similar to that of its equivalent in the United States. Among the subdivisions of the amorphous department are those dealing with: general culture, science and the arts (a division which includes the Swiss Federal Institute of Technology); inspection of public works; inspection of forests, hunting, and fishing; the federal public hygiene service; and the federal office of social insurance.

Another amorphous department is that of Finance and Customs. Among its subdivisions are: the finance administration; financial control; the bureau of weights and measures; the tax administration; the customs administration; the alcohol monopoly; the federal administration of wheat; and the secretariat of the federal bank commission. The Department of Public Economy is given very important tasks in times of economic crisis or war. During World War II, for instance, the Federal Service for the Control of Prices was under its wing. In normal times it is subdivided into: a secretariat; a division of commerce; a federal office of industry, arts and crafts, and labor; a division of agriculture; and the federal veterinary office. One of the larger departments is that of the Posts and Railways. Its size is due, of course, to the fact that the Swiss national government owns and manages the post office, telegraphs and telephones, radio and television, and the greater part of the railway system. The Post and Railway Department also is responsible for aviation and federal waterways. Besides military affairs, the Military Department is responsible for the Federal School of Gymnastics and Sport. Finally, there is the Department of Justice and Police which, in addition to its normal duties, is charged with the protection of patents and copyrights.

Federal Employees

Because the cantons are entrusted with the execution of many federal laws, the number of federal employees is not large. In 1962 there were only 110,884 people on the federal payroll, of which 80,471 were employed by the Swiss Federal Railways and the Post, Telegraph and Telephone Administration. The central administration employed only about 25,196.

The Federal Council makes all appointments with the exception of those offices which are entrusted by federal law to the Federal Assembly, the Federal Tribunal, or other federal authorities such as the Federal Railways Administration. In practice, the nomination and promotion of many federal employees is delegated by the Federal Council of the various departments. Each vacant post is advertised along with a brief job description.

"It is an absolute principle of federal administrative law that no functionary is appointed for life."[11] All appointments are for an "administrative period" usually of four years. Although in principle the service of any employee may be terminated after that period, as a general rule he is reappointed until he reaches the retirement age of sixty-five unless he should be guilty of some serious offense. At the age of sixty-five, the employee receives a pension for life based on his years of service and his annual salary. Salaries in the Swiss federal service, it should be noted, are notoriously low.

The Federal Chancellery

There is one other federal organ that should be mentioned at this point — the Federal Chancellery. The Federal Chancellery is the secretariat of the Federal Council and the Federal Assembly. Among its specific duties are supervising the publication of legal acts of the Federal Council and the Assembly, translating and keeping in custody official documents, and technically organizing federal elections and initiative and referendum votes. Certain laws and ordinances require the signature of the head of the Federal Chancellery along with that of the President of the Confederation as an attestation of their authenticity.

At the head of the Federal Chancellery is the Federal Chancellor elected by the Federal Assembly for a four-year term at the same time as the elections are held for the members of the Federal Council. In practice, he remains in office until he retires. He has one or more Vice Chancellors and a staff to aid him in his duties. In 1958 the total staff of the Chancellor numbered twenty.[12]

In view of the fact that the Federal Chancellery is the oldest organ of the government, created in 1803 to act as the secretariat of the Diet

[11] Bridel, *Précis* . . ., p. 163.
[12] Chancellerie fédérale, *Annuaire de la Confédération suisse*, 1958, p. 12.

of the Old Confederation, the Federal Chancellor is designated by the Constitution as one of the "higher federal authorities." In fact he is no more than a senior federal employee. He is not responsible to one of the federal departments, but directly to the Federal Councillor who is acting as the President of the Confederation.

Developments and Remedies

Only two changes in the form of the Swiss federal executive have been seriously considered since its creation in 1848: to choose the Federal Councillors by direct election and to increase their number. Both were defeated. The arguments for increasing the number of Councillors was based primarily on geographical considerations. It was felt that a larger number would provide for a better geographical representation. It is interesting to note that the framers of the 1848 Constitution raised the number from five to seven for the very same reason. The arguments for selecting the members by popular election were ostensibly based on the desire for a more democratic procedure. In actual fact, there were political parties or geographical areas that wanted to be represented on the Council. Although the two initiatives to achieve this were turned down, as pointed out by Hughes, in both cases the groups involved achieved their aim.[13] Whether an enlarged Federal Council, or one that is popularly elected, would maintain the desired characteristics of collegiate responsibility is open to question.

Far more important have been the suggestions to decrease the work load of the Federal Council, a load that has increased throughout the years. These suggestions became quite pertinent in 1959 when three Federal Councillors were forced to resign because of ill health. It was generally agreed that the cause was primarily the heavy responsibilities of the office.

Some successes have been achieved in this respect. In 1914 and 1929 the Federal Tribunal was given authority over certain disputes that had gone to the Federal Council in the past. More recently, the Federal Council has been given the right to let subordinates make some of the decisions that the Councillors themselves usually make. At the present time there is a move afoot to permit the Federal Councillors to send subordinates to see bills through the legislature. It is almost certain, however, that the work load of the members of the Federal Council will remain an object of concern. The procedure of giving subordinates the responsibility of making lesser decisions cannot do more than provide a temporary relief in view of the steady growth of executive responsibilities. Even if it should be decided that the Federal Council

[13] Hughes, p. 108.

may send subordinates to see bills through parliament, it is doubtful that the legislature would permit an extensive use of such an arrangement, or whether the Council itself would use it, especially when important bills are being discussed.

There are several reasons why the Swiss have permitted the Federal Council to assume more and more governmental functions. In the first place, the Council's small size makes it able to act quickly and efficiently, results that are considered desirable in modern times. Secondly, as a rule the body is well qualified to deal with governmental problems. Most members are chosen originally from the leadership of their parties in parliament, thus reflecting long terms of service at various levels of government and experience in assuming responsibility. This expertise is increased to a high degree by the custom of re-electing individuals to the Council as long as they wish to serve. This custom, it should be noted, also provides for continuity in the direction of governmental affairs.

None of these reasons would be adequate, however, if the Federal Council had not achieved for itself a reputation for acting as the true representative of the national interest. This is partially a result of its collegiate character which permits the individuals to work to a great extent anonymously. To a larger degree it is due to the manner in which the individual Councillors comport themselves once in office. So well do most devote themselves to their tasks, that almost immediately after election they become disassociated in the public mind with their former positions of leadership in political parties and even to a degree with citizenship of any certain canton. The same thing is not necessarily true for deputies of the two legislative houses. This reputation is so strong that quite often it is the Federal Assembly which receives the blame for legislation that the people reject in referendum, even though the draft was the work of the Federal Council and the legislature had done little or nothing in the way of revising its provisions.

Consequently, it can be concluded that little opposition to an even greater increase in the relative importance of the Swiss executive is likely to emerge as long as no member, or group of members, should act in a manner that would shatter its public image.

7

The Federal Tribunal

The third principal organ of the Swiss federal government is the Federal Tribunal, the highest court in Switzerland. Switzerland does not have a system of federal courts existing alongside a system of cantonal courts. Cantonal courts are entrusted with the enforcement of both federal and cantonal law. Switzerland has been content with the creation of a single high federal court to act as the final court of appeals in cases involving federal law that come to it from cantonal courts and to act as a court of original and ultimate jurisdiction in certain issues that arise from the nature of a federal government. In addition, the Federal Tribunal does not have the power, either directly or by implication, to rule on the constitutionality of federal laws.

This chapter will deal primarily with the Federal Tribunal. However, because they are essential units of the Swiss federal legal system, a section will be devoted to the structure and jurisdiction of cantonal courts as well.

Historical Development

Although created by the 1848 Constitution, the Federal Tribunal did not achieve any real prominence until it was reorganized and its duties were expanded by the 1874 constitutional revision. Before 1874, the Federal Tribunal was composed of eleven members and eleven alternates elected by the Federal Assembly for three-year terms. Judges had no regular place of meeting, and received no salary; a modest per diem was paid to them for the time spent at work. There were no qualifications for election, and the only restriction on outside interests was that judges could not be members of the Federal Council, nor could they hold an office for which the Federal Council held the power of appointment. The Federal Tribunal usually met in Berne at the same time as the federal legislature (of which many of the Tribunal judges also were members).

The jurisdiction of the Tribunal was confined to matters that were deemed beneath the dignity of either the Federal Assembly or the Federal Council. It had no jurisdiction, for instance, over conflicts in public law between the Confederation and the cantons, or between cantons. Cases of this kind were dealt with by the legislature or executive. The Federal Tribunal could settle cases in civil law between the Confederation and cantons only when and if referred by the Federal Assembly or the Federal Council. Similarly, complaints of violations of individual rights came before the Tribunal only when assigned by the legislature. As stated by Professor Rappard: "In all but one single instance, however, from 1848 until 1874, they were dealt with finally by the Federal Assembly."[1] The Federal Tribunal was left with the task of deciding a limited number of cases involving civil and criminal law, and very few of the latter, a pursuit which did not tax the ability of these amateur judges or keep them long from their other occupations.

The 1874 constitutional revision elevated the Federal Tribunal to a more respected place in the Swiss federal system. Especially important was the strengthening of organization. Federal judgeships were made career occupations by awarding regular salaries and by making tenure incompatible with other occupations. The Court was given a permanent seat in Lausanne, and a special building was erected to house it. Lausanne, in the canton of Vaud, was chosen as a concession to the French-speaking Swiss and to remove the court from the political atmosphere of Berne. The jurisdiction of the court was extended, especially in public law. Article 113, section 3, of the revised Constitution specifically gave the Federal Tribunal jurisdiction in regard to "complaints in respect of violation of constitutional rights of citizens, and complaints by individuals in respect of violation of concordats and treaties." Although the federal political authorities still had a great deal of authority over certain constitutional rights, the Tribunal's share was large.

The Federal Tribunal's jurisdiction has grown without abatement since 1874. In 1893 the federal political authorities relinquished to the Tribunal a greater number of constitutional law cases. In 1889 it was given jurisdiction over cases in debt and bankruptcy, and in 1929 over certain cases in administrative law. Two constitutional amendments adopted in 1898 gave the Federal Assembly the right to legislate on civil and criminal law. As the legislature adopted laws to carry out

[1] Rappard, *The Government of Switzerland*, p. 89.

its right the Federal Tribunal was given the task of insuring uniform enforcement. Especially important in this respect were the Swiss Civil Code of 1907 and the Swiss Criminal Code of 1937.

Composition

The Federal Tribunal is made up of twenty-six judges and twelve alternates. Judges and alternates are elected by the Federal Assembly for six-year terms. They are indefinitely eligible for re-election and are almost always re-elected for as long as they desire to remain in office. There is no age limit for service on the Federal Tribunal, but in practice judges resign the year in which they become seventy. The number of judges and alternates has been increased since the fixing of the number of judges was left to the Federal Assembly in the 1874 constitutional revision. Originally only nine judges (by the decision of the federal legislature in 1874), their number was raised to fourteen in 1893, to sixteen in 1896, to nineteen in 1904, to twenty-four in 1911, and to the present number of twenty-six in 1928. The number of alternates remained at nine from 1874 until 1943, in which year it was raised to the present level of twelve. The pertinent law now in force actually provides for "from twenty-six to twenty-eight judges and from eleven to thirteen alternates."[2]

Any Swiss citizen eligible for election to the National Council is eligible to serve on the Federal Tribunal, with the exception of members of the Federal Assembly, the Federal Council, and federal employees appointed by the Federal Council. Although there is nothing in the Constitution or federal law concerning qualifications, the Federal Assembly regularly appoints members of the legal profession, both practicing lawyers and judges of cantonal courts, professors of law, and at times other senior officials of the Federal Tribunal. The Constitution does provide, however, that in its appointments the Federal Assembly must make certain that all three official languages are represented. In practice, the Federal Assembly not only does this, but often designates more judges representing the French and Italian languages than a strict arithmetic proportion would warrant. Besides, the Federal Assembly usually makes sure that the composition of the Federal Tribunal also reflects the strength of the major political parties and the two major religions.[3]

In contrast to the situation existing before 1874, Federal judges may not exercise any other function that would be incompatible with their work. This includes "any other official duty or function in the service

[2] *Loi fédérale d'organisation judiciaire,* December 16, 1943, Art. 1.
[3] Bridel, *Précis . . ., p.* 255.

of the Confederation or a canton," any other career or profession, and any post of responsibility in a profit-making enterprise.[4] Federal law also lays down certain restrictions as to family ties between members, similar to those mentioned for the Federal Council.

Federal judges are paid a salary of 53,000 Swiss francs a year. The President of the Federal Tribunal receives an extra allowance of 3,600 and the Vice-President of 2,400. Alternates are paid a per diem for the time that they are called to serve. All judges must live in Lausanne or its general area, but they retain their civil and political rights in their canton of origin.

Jurisdiction

The jurisdiction of the Federal Tribunal is wide indeed. It is the highest court for matters of constitutional and administrative law except where controversies remain within the province of federal political authorities. It is the highest tribunal in the land for cases in civil law, and has extensive jurisdiction in matters concerning debts and bankruptcy. In criminal matters it is the court of ultimate appeal and the court that decides alone in certain cases involving high criminal offenses. The jurisdiction of the Federal Tribunal is also extremely complicated; some half a dozen laws mention the court and its tasks. An attempt to sort out the jurisdiction of the Tribunal in a systematic manner would be beyond the scope of this work and would have no more than a marginal interest for the student of the Swiss federal system.[5] Consequently, this section will be restricted to a review of the major principles of the Swiss federal jurisprudence.

First, the primary task of the Federal Tribunal is to ensure the uniform application of federal law. As the federal legislature has used its constitutional grants of power to establish single uniform codes of justice, most law has become federal law. As there are no inferior federal courts, the cases it decides come to it directly from the courts of all twenty-two cantons. In an effort to hold down the number of cases with which the Federal Tribunal might have to deal, however, cantonal courts are given final jurisdiction over many cases of lesser importance. In civil law, for example, it is a general rule that only

[4] *Loi fédérale d'organisation judiciaire,* Art. 3.

[5] In addition to Articles 106 to 114 of the federal Constitution, the following are some of the more pertinent documents now in force: *Loi fédérale d'organisation judiciaire,* December 16, 1943; *Loi fédérale de procédure civile fédérale,* December 4, 1947; *Loi fédérale sur la procédure pénale,* June 15, 1934; and *Règlement du Tribunal fédéral,* October 21, 1944. One should also consult the law of 1889 on suits for debt and bankruptcy, and the civil and criminal codes.

those cases involving sums in excess of 8,000 francs may be appealed to the Federal Tribunal. Of the average of about 2,000 cases tried annually by the high court, the overwhelming majority come on appeal.

Second, the Federal Tribunal is given original jurisdiction over important cases in the various fields of law under its authority. In matters of civil law, for instance, the Tribunal has original jurisdiction over cases between: (1) the Confederation and cantons; (2) canton and canton; (3) individuals and the Confederation when the amount in litigation exceeds 8,000 Swiss francs; (4) individuals and cantons when the amount involved is more than 8,000 francs; and (5) individuals where the amount in litigation exceeds 10,000 francs and when the two parties request the Tribunal to take jurisdiction. In the criminal area, the Federal Tribunal retains original and exclusive jurisdiction over serious offenses involving high treason and revolution, crimes against international law, actions which cause armed federal intervention, and criminal charges against appointed federal officials if referred to the court. The Tribunal also has original jurisdiction over other serious crimes such as counterfeiting and voting frauds. Cases of original jurisdiction, however make up a very small proportion of the work load of the Federal Tribunal.

Third, the federal judicial power is shared to a certain extent with other federal organs. While this sharing has been diminished appreciably over the years, it still remains, especially in the field of administrative law, and to a lesser extent in constitutional law. Thus Article 124 of the 1943 law on judicial organization provides for appeals to the *Federal Council,* rather than the Federal Tribunal, against decisions of: (1) departments of the Federal Council except where such decisions are final; (2) the highest organ of the federal railway system where expressly provided by law; and (3) certain independent federal administrative authorities. Article 125 of the same law provides for appeals to the *Federal Council* against acts and decisions of cantonal authorities concerning a few provisions of the federal Constitution, notably: Article 18, para. 3 (free military equipment); Article 27, paras. 2 and 3 (nature of primary school education); Article 51 (prohibition of Jesuits); and Article 53, para. 2 (cemeteries). Some decisions of the Federal Council in the field of public and administrative law can be appealed to the Federal Assembly. Article 96 of the same law requires that the Tribunal and Council meet to discuss cases where there is a doubt as to which body has jurisdiction. The Federal Tribunal also shares certain restricted areas of judicial power with the Federal Insurance Tribunal and the military authorities.

Fourth, the Federal Tribunal exercises the important function of guaranteeing to the individual his constitutional rights. This includes most of the rights guaranteed in the Federal Constitution as well as those guaranteed by the cantonal constitutions. With certain exceptions, such as cases involving the right of establishment and double taxation, appeals will not be accepted by the Federal Tribunal unless the individual in question has exhausted cantonal remedies. It should be noted, however, that this protection is provided mainly against actions of cantonal governments and not the federal government. The Federal Tribunal can invalidate cantonal laws and it can inquire into the constitutionality of actions of cantonal executive officials. In practice, there are a great number of such appeals brought before the Federal Tribunal each year, the great majority of which concern Article 4 of the Constitution, which guarantees equality before the law.

Fifth, as implicit in the preceding discussion, the Federal Tribunal does not have the power to inquire into the constitutionality of a federal law or treaty. Its power of judicial review is confined to cantonal laws and to actions by cantonal and sometimes federal executives. However, as pointed out by Professor Hans Huber, at one time a judge of the Federal Tribunal, the court will make an effort to interpret federal statutes whose meaning is not clear in such a manner as to honor the intent of the Constitution.[6]

Finally, in all cases of a conflict between cantonal law and federal law, it is the latter which prevails. This principle is important mainly in spheres of public and administrative law.

Organization and Procedure

The Federal Tribunal meets in plenary session only for the purpose of deciding on questions involving substantive conflict between its various subdivisions, making nominations, making administrative decisions, and adopting internal rules and regulations. Other matters may be brought before the entire membership of the court if federal law or the court's own regulations should so determine.

For the actual judging of cases, the Federal Tribunal is subdivided into several principal courts specializing in the major spheres of law. There is a Court of Constitutional and Administrative Law of nine judges, which is further subdivided into a Chamber of Constitutional Law and a Chamber of Administrative Law. All nine judges are members of the former and five are also members of the latter. There are two Civil Law Courts, of six members each, and a Court of Criminal Appeals composed of five judges. Each of the twenty-six federal judges is assigned to one of these principal courts.

[6] See W. G. Rice, *Law Among States in Federacy* (Appleton, Wisconsin: C. C. Nelson, 1959), p. 117.

The Federal Tribunal also has several lesser chambers. For each of the judges sitting on one of these, the appointment may be their second or third. There is a Chamber of Debts and Bankruptcy (*Chambre des poursuites et des faillites*) of three judges. There is also a group of chambers whose major task is to try the infrequent cases where the Tribunal has original criminal jurisdiction, composed of a Chamber of Accusation of three judges (*Chambre d'accusation*), the Criminal Chamber of three judges representing the three official languages (*Chambre criminelle*), and the Federal Penal Court composed of five judges, three from the Criminal Chamber and two others (*Cour pénale fédérale*). When the three members of the Criminal Chamber sit with a jury to try cases, it is known as the Federal Assizes (*Assises fédérales*).[7] There is also a provision for an Extraordinary Court of Cassation that may be called to review the judgments of the Federal Assizes, the Criminal Chamber, and the Federal Penal Court, and to decide on conflicts of jurisdiction between the Federal Assizes and the Federal Penal Court. This special court is formed of the President and Vice-President of the Federal Tribunal and five of the Tribunal's oldest members who are not members of the Chamber of Accusation or the Federal Penal Court.

Even in criminal cases where the Federal Tribunal has original and exclusive jurisdiction, federal law recognizes the distinction between indictment for a crime and judgment for a crime. To aid it in the first of the two processes, the Tribunal has access to the services of the Procurer General, the federal criminal police, and three Instructional Judges. The Procurer General, who holds a place in the Swiss system similar to that of the Attorney General in the American system, is appointed by the Federal Council and operates within the Department of Justice and Police. The Instructional Judges, one for each of the major linguistic divisions, are appointed by the Tribunal for six-year terms. Inasmuch as the original jurisdiction of the Federal Tribunal does not give rise to a great number of cases, the Instructional Judges may also hold outside employment.

If the federal criminal police uncover evidence of a crime for which the Federal Tribunal has original jurisdiction, the Procurer General may instruct one of the Instructional Judges to open an investigation.

[7] The juries that sit with the Criminal Chamber to try grave criminal cases are elected by the people for six-year terms, on the basis of one juror for each 3,000 inhabitants. They are elected from each of three districts, one for the French- and Italian-speaking cantons and two for the German-speaking cantons. All Swiss who are eligible to vote in federal matters are liable for duty on a federal jury with the exception of cantonal and federal administrative and judicial personnel and those exercising ecclesiastical functions. Those over the age of sixty or who are too ill to serve may be excused.

If the Instructional Judge deems that the evidence placed at his disposal by the Procurer General warrants it, he undertakes an investigation, notifying the Court of Accusation of the action. The Judge of Instruction may take testimony and call witnesses to testify before him. If the Procurer General decides that the investigation uncovers a sufficient presumption of guilt, he makes out an "act of accusation" and communicates it together with the files on the case to the Chamber of Accusation. The Chamber in turn opens an investigation. The court can request the Instructional Judge to gather further evidence or otherwise revise the results of his preliminary investigation. If the Chamber of Accusation comes to the conclusion that a crime has been committed, and that the Federal Tribunal has jurisdiction, it turns the completed files over to either the Federal Assizes or the Federal Penal Court for judging. Article 112 of the Constitution specifies that the Federal Assizes must judge all cases involving: high treason, rebellion, or violence against federal authorities; crimes against international law; crimes which give rise to federal intervention; and criminal charges against federal appointed officials if referred to the court.

The Federal Tribunal has a President and a Vice-President appointed by the Federal Assembly from among the members of the Tribunal itself, for a period of two years. The President assumes the general direction of Tribunal affairs and supervises its officers and employees. In the case of impeachment, the Vice-President assumes the President's duties. In the event both men are impeached, the President's duties fall on the shoulders of the member with the longest service. If there should be more than one member with the same length of service, the oldest takes charge. The number of clerks and secretaries of the Federal Tribunal is fixed by the Federal Assembly, but the Tribunal nominates its staff and determines their actual functions.

The procedural rules of the Federal Tribunal are neither extensive nor exceedingly restrictive. All the Presidents of the various sections of the court are designated by the Federal Tribunal in plenary session except those of the Penal Court and the Criminal Chamber. These two nominate their own presidents for each case. A quorum of two-thirds of the membership is necessary for the Federal Tribunal meeting in plenary session and the Court of Constitutional Law must have seven judges available except when judging cases under Article 4 of the Constitution, at which time five is a quorum. For the other courts and chambers the quorum is five judges or fewer as determined by law. As a general rule decisions in the courts and chambers are made by a majority vote and the president of the unit is given the deciding vote in the case of a tie. Most hearings, including the deliberations of the judges and voting, are open to the public. Exceptions are made for the deliberations and voting in criminal divisions, for the Chamber of Administrative Law in disciplinary cases, and for the Chamber of Debts and Bankruptcy. Further, the Federal Tribunal can order a private hearing when it considers it essential to public security, order, and decency, or when the interests of a party make it necessary.

The regulations of the Tribunal provide that a judge must disqualify himself in any case involving a personal interest, an interest of a relative (including fiancées and those related up to the fourth degree), a previous official responsibility, the canton or commune of origin of the judge, or a relationship between the judge and an attorney representing one of the parties.

The judges on the Federal Tribunal have no special dress for their work. Article 15 of the Rules of Procedure states simply: "The judges, as well as the clerks and secretaries, shall wear black clothes when appearing in public sittings." The same rule holds true for the lawyers representing the parties before the court. It is interesting to note that the judges on the Federal Tribunal do not write their own opinions. After both written and oral testimony have been presented — the latter only if permitted — each judge sitting on the case presents his opinion orally. The clerk of the court takes notes on the judges' statements and, after they have finished, draws up the official opinion of the court.[8]

Table 9

Cases Judged by the Federal Tribunal in 1962

Type of Case	Number
1. Civil Law (original jurisdiction — 7)	335
2. Criminal Law	488
3. Constitutional Law	661
4. Administrative Law	112
5. Debts and Bankruptcy	118
6. Other	2
Total	1,716

Other Judicial Bodies

There is one federal court that does not fit into the Federal Tribunal system, the Federal Insurance Court. In contrast to its actions in regard

[8] For further information concerning the procedure of the Federal Tribunal, both formal and informal, see Rice, pp. 110–114.

to the proposed Court of Administrative Law, the Federal Assembly made the Federal Insurance Court autonomous and independent of the Federal Tribunal. The Federal Insurance Court, situated in Lucerne, hears appeals from the cantonal insurance courts concerning the application of social insurance laws including health and accident insurance, military insurance, and old age and survivors' insurance. The Insurance Court is composed of five judges and five alternates, elected by the Federal Assembly.

In addition to the Insurance Court and the Federal Tribunal, the Swiss have also provided for special military tribunals to apply the military criminal code. There are several courts of the first instance organized on a divisional or territorial basis and one Court of Military Appeals. All such courts are made up of military personnel with special training.[9]

Cantonal Courts

Because cantons are given the responsibility of enforcing federal law, the cantonal courts are essential parts of the federal legal system. Cantonal courts apply most federal law in the first and second instance, leaving to the Federal Tribunal final appellate jurisdiction. Since the introduction of a single national code for civil, commercial, and criminal law, the law applied by cantons has been uniform. The structure of the court system, however, is left to the cantons to determine. Consequently, there can be, and is, quite a divergence between the practices followed by the cantons.

In most cantons there are three levels of justice in civil law: the justices of the peace, the district courts, and a superior cantonal court. In civil cases, the amount involved in litigation and the nature of the case determines whether the justice of the peace, the district court, or the highest cantonal court has original jurisdiction. The justice of the peace has the duty of attempting to settle every controversy that comes before him by arbitration (in some cantons his title is "mediator" — *Vermittler*). Only after failure of arbitration does he try the case. The district courts, which take more serious cases, are made up from five to seven judges, including a President and a Vice-President. While there is usually a justice of the peace for every commune, the district court's authority extends over a much wider area, such as a district or an arrondissement. The district courts may decide cases in plenary session or in smaller groups. In most cantons there is a single high court whose jurisdiction extends over the whole territory of the can-

[9] See Bridel, p. 267 and Sauser-Hall, *Guide politique suisse,* p. 165. The Swiss also have several federal administrative courts.

ton. This court is essentially a court of review except in certain classes of cases, such as those regarding industrial property, where federal law gives it original and unique jurisdiction. Most high cantonal courts are composed of five or more members and are broken up into subdivisions to try the cases that come before them.

The organization of courts is slightly different for criminal cases. The lowest criminal authority is the police tribunal, the police judge, and in some cantons the Justice of the Peace. The next level of justice is the district court, usually the same as for civil cases, and finally the single high cantonal court. Whether a case goes to the police judge, the district court, or the high court depends usually on the gravity of the crime. Police judges have the power to inflict fines and short jail sentences, the district court to judge misdemeanors and to inflict longer prison sentences. The high cantonal courts judge serious crimes and have the power to inflict even longer sentences. In the canton of Neuchâtel, the police judge can imprison a person for a maximum of three months, the district court for three years, and the criminal section of the highest court for longer terms.[10] From this court, of course, appeal can in most cases be made to the Federal Tribunal.

Cantonal judges are for the most part elected directly either by the people or by the cantonal legislature. There are usually no special qualifications for cantonal judgeship except for service on the highest court. The cantons decide the terms of judges, and in most instances judges may be re-elected as long as they wish to serve.[11]

⁕

Of the three major federal organs, the Federal Tribunal was the longest in attaining its full stature. While the other organs were performing essential functions since 1848, the Tribunal was not given any important powers until the constitutional revision of 1874. Starting with the grant of jurisdiction over cases involving constitutional rights in 1874, the powers of the Tribunal have increased without let-up.

At the present time it is eminently worthy of its place as the highest court of the land. It performs essential functions in the unification of law and in guarding the constitutional rights of Swiss citizens. As a system, one federal court standing directly over the cantonal courts, it seems to work well and without any undue friction. The benefits of a single standard of justice in most fields of law outweigh the resultant invasion of cantonal authority. There are without doubt many in the

[10] Bridel, p. 231.
[11] For further information on the organization and jurisdiction of cantonal courts, see Bridel, pp. 215–250.

United States who would welcome a similar transformation in American law. It should be noted, however, that the Swiss system was achieved only by leaving the lower levels of justice with the cantons.

While the stature of the Federal Tribunal will probably continue to grow, many persons feel that it is doubtful whether it ever can attain that of the United States Supreme Court. Many reasons are given for this conclusion. One is that the large size of the Tribunal and the small size of the Swiss population make it less attractive to the top legal minds than is the case with its counterpart in the United States. On the other hand, it can be argued that the Tribunal, at least in the past fifty years, has attracted top legal talent, more so, perhaps, than the United States Supreme Court. Another reason given is that the Swiss judges are appointed for specific terms, rather than for life and good behavior as in the United States. Nevertheless, the Swiss practice of re-electing judges as long as they want to serve seems to have overcome the evils that such a system could create. Another point raised is that the Tribunal still shares some of the federal judicial functions with other federal authorities. However, in practice this is not very significant, and the institution of a single criminal and civil code actually gives it a wider degree of jurisdiction than its sister organ in the United States. In addition, there is the controversial argument that the Federal Tribunal has not always stood up to the Swiss executive when the latter has acted in a manner that seems to the critics to be contrary to individual statutory and constitutional rights.[12]

The basic reason why the Federal Tribunal does not have a status equal to that of the United States Supreme Court, however, is that it does not have the right to declare federal laws unconstitutional. The giving of such authority to the Tribunal has been the subject of discussion among very competent people for years, but it has never had the support of a real popular movement. The one time it was brought before the people in 1939, by popular initiative, it was decisively rejected. The opponents feel that such an extension of authority would be undemocratic, preferring to cling to the concept of legislative supremacy, and, with the legislative referendum by which no major law can become effective without the tacit or express approval of the people, unnecessary.

[12] See Rice, pp. 110–114.

⌗ *8* ⌗

Political Parties and Interest Groups

In many ways, the political party system in Switzerland is analogous to that found in the United States. It performs the same essential functions of organizing and stimulating public opinion, defining political issues, and presenting candidates for positions in the various organs of government. Parties are also similar in that both are loose federations of local party organizations. Swiss political parties are not recognized in the country's basic documents, except indirectly in the laws governing the legislative organization and procedure, and in the electoral laws.

The most important difference between the two is the multi-party nature of the Swiss system. There are three major parties with almost equal control over the Federal Assembly and the Federal Council. There is one significant smaller party whose views cannot be ignored and a group of lesser ones. Because there are no extreme differences in the philosophy and social composition of the Swiss parties and because the Swiss love for order and compromise is as strong in politics as it is elsewhere, this situation has not led to the instability that is found among two of Switzerland's close neighbors.[1]

[1] The following is a list of the names of the seven national parties that will be discussed in this chapter, including the names as they are used in this text and their present official French and German equivalents. As will be explained later, the names of the national parties are not necessarily the same as those of affiliated cantonal parties.
a. Radical party

After a discussion of the history, policies, and structure of Swiss political parties, interest group activity will also be treated. The purpose of interest group activity in Switzerland is basically the same as it is elsewhere. As will be seen, however, the Swiss political system tends to provide more opportunities for the open and direct participation of interest groups in the political process than does the system in the United States, for example.

Evolution of Swiss Political Parties

The history of Swiss political parties under the federal system can be described in terms of the rise and fall of the Radical party. From the institution of the Constitution of 1848 to 1919, the Radical party was in full control of the government in Berne. After the introduction of proportional representation for elections to the National Council in 1919, however, the Radical party dropped from a place of dominance to one of a strong party in a multi-party system. By 1935 it had lost its plurality in the Council of States, by 1955 in the National Council, and by 1959 in the Federal Council. Since 1959, Switzerland has enjoyed a true multi-party representation in all of the key organs of government.

Before 1848 there were only three Swiss political parties, the Liberals, Radicals, and Catholics. The Liberal party was the creation of a group of intellectuals, workers, and farmers who were dissatisfied with the restoration of feudal privileges by the Pact of 1815. The activities of the Liberal party reached their climax with the triumph

---

    1) Parti radical-démocratique suisse
    2) Freisinnig-demokratische Partei der Schweiz
b. Catholic Conservative party
    1) Parti conservateur et chrétien-social de la Suisse
    2) Konservativ-christlichsoziale Volkspartei der Schweiz
c. Socialist party
    1) Parti social-démocrate suisse
    2) Sozialdemokratischen Partei der Schweiz
d. Farmers party
    1) Parti suisse des paysans, artisans et bourgeois
    2) Schweizerische Bauern-, Gewerbe- und Bürgerpartei
e. Independent party
    1) Parti indépendant
    2) Landesring der Unabhängigen
f. Liberal party
    1) Parti libéral suisse
    2) Liberale Partei der Schweiz
g. Communist party
    1) Parti suisse du travail
    2) Partei der Arbeit der Schweiz

of individual and political liberties in a majority of cantons in the 1830's. In 1832 the "liberal wing" of the Liberal party broke away and organized the Radical party to carry the revolution one step further: the establishment of a strong democratic national state that would guarantee liberal principles throughout Switzerland. The Catholic party was organized in the 1830's to oppose both the Liberals and the Radicals. It wanted no change in the Pact of 1815 for fear of interference in cantonal affairs and, by implication, in religious affairs. As noted earlier, this fear grew so strong that it led to the Sonderbund War. After the war, the Liberals and the Radicals pooled their resources to create the Constitution of 1848.

The federal Constitution was inaugurated in 1848 with the Liberals and Radicals controlling the major organs of government. Only a few Catholics, lucky enough to be elected despite the liberal tide, were present in the National Council. The reforming spirit of the Liberals died with the Constitution of 1848, however, and it began a defensive battle, opposing, almost without exception, the innovations demanded by the Radicals. Popular support was on the side of the Radicals, and its strength increased as that of the Liberals decreased. The constitutional revision of 1874 was almost entirely the work of the predominant Radical party.

By 1890 the Radical party was in control of some eighty-three seats in the National Council while the Liberals held only twenty-two. In the Federal Council, the Radicals held six seats and the Liberals only one. That the Liberals were allowed one seat in the Federal Council was not due to their strength in the country, however, but to the custom prevailing even then of re-electing the incumbent for as long as he chose to continue in office. Actually the Catholic Conservatives, who had slowly but surely increased their representation in the National Council to thirty-five by 1890, were second in importance. In 1891 a Catholic was designated to replace the lone Liberal on the Federal Council.

1890 was also a key year for the first appearance of the Socialist party in the national political arena. Socialism had made its appearance in Switzerland in the 1830's and had been organized as a political party for the first time in Zurich in 1870. Socialist forces were too widespread, however, to permit them to elect members to the National Council until the 1890 elections. In that year six Socialists took their seats alongside the Liberals, Radicals, and Catholics.

It is difficult to pinpoint the exact date when the majority of Swiss voters became disillusioned with Radical rule. As late as 1917, just two years before the institution of proportional representation, the

Radicals maintained a majority of 108 out of 189 members of the National Council. The Catholics held only thirty-nine seats and the Socialists eighteen. The Liberals had only thirteen and the remaining eleven were distributed among minor parties. Perhaps the two most important groups that the Radicals had failed to satisfy were the farmers and the city laborers. The workers had begun to band together in syndicates in the 1870's, and the farmers had created an Agrarian party in 1897. Nonetheless, emergence of widespread dissatisfaction was not reflected in the major federal organs. The Radicals were still powerful enough, until 1919, to achieve a strong plurality in a majority of the elections for the National Council.

The introduction of proportional representation in 1919 brought the Radical party down to earth. The Radicals twice defeated proportional referendum initiatives, both in November of 1900 and in October, 1910, but failed in October, 1918, when 299,550 voters and $19\frac{1}{2}$ cantons voted in favor and only 149,035 voters and $2\frac{1}{2}$ cantons voted against. All the other parties supported the successful initiative both from the viewpoint of a genuine desire for reform — many cantons and communes had already initiated it — and from a desire to end the Radicals' one-party rule.

As a result of the 1919 elections, held under the new rules of proportional representation, the Swiss political party system took on a multi-party aspect that has endured to this day. The heaviest loser was the Radical party, which lost forty-five of its 108 seats in the National Council. The greatest gainer was the Socialist party, which jumped from eighteen to forty-one. The Catholic party was not severely affected one way or another, picking up two seats to bring up its effectives also to forty-one. The old Liberal party emerged with only nine representatives. The Farmers, Artisans, and Citizens party, a new one dedicated to the welfare of the Swiss farmers and made up of former members of the Radical party, entered the new multi-party epoch with twenty-five National Councillors.

The period from 1919 to 1959 was not noted for any significant change in the composition of the National Council. The Catholics, Radicals, and Socialists achieved a parity of representation that did not affect more than a few seats either way. The Radicals lost their plurality, but no other party rose to replace it. Two new parties came into existence, the Independent party and the Communist party. The Independents, devoted to the elimination of government control over the economy, achieved the position of fifth largest party, but a poor fifth. The Communists, on the other hand, devoted to a diametrically opposed view, made a consistently poor showing.

The representation of the parties in the Council of States, with its more conservative methods of election, did not show any important changes in the 1919–1959 period with the possible exception of the Radicals' loss of a plurality to the Catholics.

As a result of the method of selecting its members, and the custom of allowing members to continue in office as long as they wished, the Federal Council was slower to reflect the true strength of Swiss political parties. Starting with five Radicals and two Catholics after the elections of 1919, ten years elapsed before the composition of the Council changed. In 1929 one Radical retired to be replaced by a member of the Farmers party. Despite the fact that the Socialists had been as strong as the Catholics in national elections, not until 1943 were the middle-class parties willing to accept a Socialist in the Swiss executive. The new "tradition" that many felt had been inaugurated by this action was rudely interrupted when the Socialist, Dr. Max Weber, head of the Federal Finance Department, resigned. His proposal for the legalization of direct federal taxation was rejected by a referendum, and the Socialist party decided not to put forward another candidate. The vacated Socialist seat was given to the Catholic party. Consequently, in 1954 the Federal Council was made up of three Radicals, three Catholics, and one Farmers.

The Socialist withdrawal was only temporary, however. This party put up two candidates in 1959 when four members of the Council announced their resignations. After being forced to replace one of its candidates, actually the president of their party, with a more acceptable one, the Socialists obtained two seats. Consequently, in 1959, the powerful Federal Council reflected for the first time, as much as its size can, the true alignment of Swiss political party strength. In a rather spiteful, although perhaps true account of what occurred, Mr. Willy Bretscher, editor-in-chief of the Radical newspaper *Neue Zürcher Zeitung,* stated: ". . . the Catholic-Conservatives some time ago had committed themselves, in a burst of bad temper caused by a petty quarrel with the Radicals, to the formula of proportional representation of all the major parties in the Government, and they seized the opportunity to put this scheme into effect with the avowed purpose of cutting the Radicals — their historical adversaries at and since the time of the founding of the modern Swiss federal state — down to size. Thus it came to pass that the Federal Assembly, in which the Catholic-Conservatives and the Socialists muster nearly one-half of the members, filled the four vacancies in the Government according to the 'magic formula' 2:2:2:1, that is to say, by introducing two Socialists into the Federal Council."[2]

[2] Willy Bretscher, "New Government in Berne," *Swiss Review of World Affairs,* IX (January, 1960), 1.

Table 10

Party Representation in the National Council

Election Year	Catholics	Radicals	Socialists	Farmers	Independents	Liberals	Communists	Others	Total
1919	41	63	41	25	0	9	0	10	189
1922	44	58	43	35	0	10	0	8	198
1925	42	59	49	30	0	7	3	8	198
1928	46	58	50	31	0	6	0	7	198
1931	44	52	49	30	0	6	0	6	187
1935	42	48	50	21	7	7	0	12	187
1939	43	51	45	22	9	6	0	11	187
1943	43	47	56	23	5	8	0	12	194
1947	44	52	48	21	9	7	7	6	194
1951	48	51	49	23	10	5	5	5	196
1955	47	50	53	22	10	5	4	5	196
1959	47	51	51	23	10	5	3	6	196
1963	48	51	53	22	10	6	4	6	200

Table 11

Party Representation in the Council of States

Election Year	Catholics	Radicals	Socialists	Farmers	Independents	Liberals	Communists	Others	Total
1919	17	23	0	1	0	2	0	1	44
1922	17	23	1	1	0	1	0	1	44
1925	18	21	2	1	0	1	0	1	44
1928	18	20	0	3	0	1	0	2	44
1931	18	19	2	3	0	1	0	1	44
1935	19	15	3	3	0	2	0	2	44
1939	18	14	3	4	0	2	0	3	44
1943	19	12	5	4	0	2	0	2	44
1947	18	11	5	4	0	2	0	4	44
1951	18	12	4	3	0	3	0	4	44
1955	17	12	5	3	0	3	0	4	44
1959	17	13	4	3	0	3	0	4	44
1963	18	13	3	4	0	3	0	3	44

Table 12

Party Representation in the Federal Council

1848–1890	Radical-Liberal
1890	6 Radicals and 1 Liberal
1891	6 Radicals and 1 Catholic
1919	5 Radicals and 2 Catholics
1929	4 Radicals, 2 Catholics, and 1 Farmers
1943	3 Radicals, 2 Catholics, 1 Farmers, and 1 Socialist
1953	4 Radicals, 2 Catholics, and 1 Farmers
1954	3 Radicals, 3 Catholics, and 1 Farmers
1959 and 1963	2 Radicals, 2 Catholics, 2 Socialists, and 1 Farmers

Party Policies

Catholic Conservatives

The Catholic Conservative party is the major conservative group in the Swiss political spectrum. Since the Sonderbund War, its primary purpose has been to protect and preserve the doctrines and institutions of the Catholic Church, especially in the rural cantons where its strength has been greatest. In order to accomplish this aim, the Catholics have been forced into being a "cantonal rights" party, attacking all moves toward centralization of political and economic power by the federal government as well as attempting to obtain the repeal of those parts of the Swiss Constitution which restrict Church activities. Although many decades of participation in government have softened the early Catholic repugnance toward a federal state per se, its platforms usually contain exhortations against overcentralization and any increase in the federal bureaucracy.

The Catholics still make a point of being the defenders of individual liberty, which includes property rights and protection of the family, preferring to rely on the Church, private philanthropy, and cooperative institutions rather than on the state to safeguard the individual's welfare. On the other hand, the Catholic party has recently taken an increasingly benevolent attitude toward social legislation, especially in the labor field. Protection of workers' rights, family allowances, and the encouragement of labor unions and collective bargaining have all become part of the official program. This liberalization of attitude has been due almost equally to a recognition of modern social developments, to a desire to broaden the base of its electoral support, and to an acknowledgement of recent general directives from the Catholic hierarchy. The party has gone so far as to change its official name to the Christian Social Conservatives, a name, however, which few within or without the party have adopted for ordinary usage. One consequence of the attempted reorientation has been to create two rival camps, one conservative and one liberal. The traditional political-religious ideology of the Catholics provides the cement that keeps these two dissident wings together, and the overall orientation of party policy is still mainly on the side of conservatism.

The Radicals

The Radical party occupies the center of the Swiss political spectrum, somewhere between the Catholics on the right and the Socialists on the left. Its exact position depends largely on the issue at hand. On some issues it finds itself backing the Socialists against conservative Catholic policies and on others it joins cause with the Catholics to block Socialist-inspired legislation that it considers too progressive.

Its present position is far from that occupied in the early days of the Confederation. At that time it had opposition only from the right. The Radical platform called for a strong central government, social legislation, and a maximum degree of direct democracy. Its loss of position as the "radical" Swiss party has been due largely to two factors over the years: its success in getting its programs accepted and its abdication to the Socialist party of the initiative in social legislation.

Earlier programs, such as that represented by the slogan of "a single law and a single army," were realized in the constitutional reorganization of 1874 and in subsequent constitutional amendments. Under the leadership of the Radicals, direct democracy has become a reality. Whereas the Radical party still considers itself the party of a strong central government, it has not been adverse in recent years to warning the nation about the dangers inherent in any further encroachment on the powers of the cantons, and, when new powers have been granted to the government in Berne, to advocating sharing legal administration with the cantons. As regards direct democracy, its successes have left it with only one more field to conquer — that is, the introduction of a system of legislative initiative.

The same trend is true in relation to social legislation. As its programs have become a reality, the Radical party has tended to become more conservative. While still maintaining a program of social welfare, it seems to have turned the leadership in this area along with much of its working-class support over to the Socialists. Concern for individuals has been replaced to a certain degree by concern for economic groups. However, the Radical party still maintains adherents in all walks of life, especially where its middle-of-the-road appeal is reinforced by popular leadership.

About the only portion of its original program that remains for the Radicals to continue to support without compromise is the emphasis on secularism. The Radical party can always be found in opposition to any issue that would tend to increase the power of the Catholic Church or in any way reduce the freedom of religious preference.

The Socialists

Although the Swiss Socialist party is the major party of the left, it has progressively eliminated most of the extreme Marxist elements from its policies. No longer are its programs interspersed with references to the establishment of a collectivist society and the need for the conquest of political control by the workers. In their stead, the Swiss Socialists have substituted an economic credo based on individual freedom. "Every man, irrespective of his origin and possessions," reads the 1959 platform, "shall be free to develop his faculties and capacities."[3] In the main, this can be accomplished by giving the individual more voice in important economic decisions. The purpose is not to destroy capitalism, but rather to eliminate its major abuses. The Swiss Socialists are quite willing to accept a mixed economy.

Specifically, the Socialist platform advocates shorter working hours, guarantees of full employment, and the expansion of social insurance. Wherever possible minimum wages and allied fringe benefits should be achieved by collective bargaining. The state should help create a climate conducive to collective bargaining and step in only when such bargaining is not possible. The Socialists also advocate a direct federal taxing power, are the most militant backers of woman suffrage, and the only major party to advocate that Switzerland join the United Nations.

As a general rule, the Socialists have moderated their policies as they have accepted more and more responsibility in governing the affairs of Switzerland. The latest change, pointed out by the supporters of rival parties, occurred just prior to the 1959 election of two Socialists to the Federal Council. In the election, as noted earlier, the Socialists were also willing to permit the Federal Assembly to re-

[3] *Programme of the Swiss Social Democratic Party, Adopted by the Party Congress held in Winterthur on 27th–28th June, 1959*, p. 3.

place the president of the Socialist party with another much younger Socialist candidate and one who had not been involved with the party's left wing of an earlier period.

It is not outside the realm of possibility that the party may lose some of its effectives as it takes on a more middle-class orientation. Already there have been rumors of a serious conflict between those who advocate furnishing the Swiss army with nuclear weapons and those who oppose it. Further, a new party has made its appearance in the canton of Neuchâtel. It is made up of a few Communists unhappy over the role of the U.S.S.R. in Hungary and a few former Socialists who have become disgusted with the increasing conservatism of the Socialist party platform. Although its ranks are still thin, the new party, which calls itself the New Socialist Left (*Nouvelle gauche socialiste*), may indicate an important future trend.

Minor Parties

In addition to the three predominant groups, there are only two other political parties of any real significance in Switzerland, the Farmers party and the Independent party. The most important of the two is the former with its delegation of twenty-two men in the National Council and its four members in the Council of State. The stated purpose of the Farmers party is to ameliorate the conditions of the farmers, artisans, and the Swiss middle class. More important than general policy statements, however, is the activity on the part of the farmer who provides the backbone of support. While rejecting in principle any intervention by the state in the economic life of the country, it has promoted subsidies to farmers, higher tariffs on imported farm produce, and governmental fixing of prices for agricultural products.

The Independent party, organized by Gottlieb Duttweiler, the head of the first supermarket chain in Switzerland, makes up in articulation for what it lacks in actual political power. It stands for the defense of the consumer's interests and opposes all state intervention in the country's economic life. The head of the party has been known to use all possible means to bring the consumer's plight to the attention of the authorities.

Despite the fact that its position on public issues is a much watered down version of orthodox communism, the Communist party has never made much headway in Switzerland. Before being banned by the government in 1940, three was the highest number of representatives it could elect to the National Council. Since the government revoked its ban in 1945, and its name has been changed to the Labor party, the

Communists have never been able to elect more than seven deputies. In the 1960 legislature there were only four.

The Liberal party still clings to its Protestant and conservative platform despite the continued decline in adherents and membership in the National Council and the Council of States. In the winter of 1960–61, the Liberals, mostly from Basle Town, Geneva, Neuchâtel, and Vaud, reorganized under the new name of the Liberal Democratic Union of Switzerland in an attempt to stop the march towards extinction.

Geographical Distribution

The lessening of religious tensions, the blurring of differences in party philosophies, changes in social structure, and immigration from canton to canton have over the years given Swiss political parties a wide geographical distribution. This is especially so as regards the three major parties with supporters in almost every canton. The Catholics still have strong standing, however, in the cantons of Uri, Schwyz, Unterwalden, Zug, Fribourg, St. Gallen, Appenzell-Inner Rhodes, and Valais. In addition the Catholics usually run a little ahead of the Radicals and other parties in Lucerne and the Grisons. The Radicals are powerful in Vaud, Solothurn, and Thurgau, and usually can make a good showing in Geneva, Glarus, and Appenzell-Outer Rhodes, but divide Ticino with the Catholics. For the Radicals, more than the Catholics, such a breakdown of power is misleading since they usually come in a strong second or third in many more instances. The Socialists draw their largest support from the industrial areas of Zurich, Basle Town and Country, Aargau, and Neuchâtel. The Socialists also do well in Solothurn and Thurgau, but are second to the Radicals, and likewise second to the Farmers in Berne and Schaffhausen. Berne and Schaffhausen are the centers of the Farmers' support, but this group also shows slight strength in Zurich and Aargau. The other parties can claim no majorities, but the Liberals have retained some support in Vaud, Neuchâtel, Basle Town, and Geneva. The Independents gain most of their support from Zurich, and the Communists from Geneva, Vaud, Basle Town, and Zurich.

Party Organization

With the exception of the Socialist party, there are no really autonomous national parties in Switzerland. Several reasons account for this phenomenon. In the first place there are the effects of the parties' historical development. Parties were first formed in the cantons and then grouped on a national scale. For instance, although the Radicals had been active in politics since 1848, they did not form a parliamen-

Table 13

Representatives in the National Council
by Canton and by Party in 1964

Canton	Catholic Conservatives	Radicals	Socialists	Farmers	Independents	Liberals	Others	Total
Zurich	5	6	10	5	5	0	4	35
Berne	2	6	12	11	2	0	0	33
Lucerne	5	3	1	0	0	0	0	9
Uri	0	1	0	0	0	0	0	1
Schwyz	2	0	1	0	0	0	0	3
Obwalden	1	0	0	0	0	0	0	1
Nidwalden	1	0	0	0	0	0	0	1
Glarus	0	1	1	0	0	0	0	2
Zug	1	1	0	0	0	0	0	2
Fribourg	3	2	1	0	0	0	0	6
Solothurn	2	3	2	0	0	0	0	7
Basle Town	1	2	3	0	1	1	0	8
Basle Country	1	1	2	1	0	0	0	5
Schaffhausen	0	1	1	0	0	0	0	2
Appenzell- Outer Rhodes	0	1	1	0	0	0	0	2
Appenzell- Inner Rhodes	1	0	0	0	0	0	0	1
St. Gallen	6	4	2	0	1	0	0	13
Grisons	2	1	0	0	0	0	2	5
Aargau	3	3	4	2	1	0	0	13
Thurgau	1	1	2	2	0	0	0	6
Ticino	3	3	1	0	0	0	0	7
Vaud	1	6	4	1	0	2	2	16
Valais	5	1	1	0	0	0	0	7
Neuchâtel	0	2	2	0	0	1	0	5
Geneva	2	2	2	0	0	2	2	10
Total	48	51	53	22	10	6	10	200

tary group until 1878. The Catholics did not follow suit until 1881. Consequently, the party structure, policies, and even names of the cantonal parties depended primarily upon the personality of the local organizers. In the second place, the road to political office and political fame is a cantonal road. To a great extent the Swiss are parochial in outlook, and the affairs of the canton play a key, perhaps even exaggerated, role in everyday life. This attitude has been kept alive in recent years by the federal government's practice of sharing with the cantons the administration of federal affairs. To be elected to the cantonal parliament or to become an important cantonal administrator are no mean achievements and carry a great deal of esteem. From a purely practical point of view, many individuals can no longer afford to spend the time demanded by the increasing length of the unpaid

Table 14

Representatives in the Council of States by Canton and by Party in 1963

Canton	Catholic Conservatives	Radicals	Socialists	Farmers	Independents	Liberals	Others	Total
Zurich	0	0	1	1	0	0	0	2
Berne	0	1	0	1	0	0	0	2
Lucerne	1	1	0	0	0	0	0	2
Uri	2	0	0	0	0	0	0	2
Schwyz	2	0	0	0	0	0	0	2
Obwalden	1	0	0	0	0	0	0	1
Nidwalden	1	0	0	0	0	0	0	1
Glarus	0	0	0	0	0	0	2	2
Zug	2	0	0	0	0	0	0	2
Fribourg	2	0	0	0	0	0	0	2
Solothurn	0	1	1	0	0	0	0	2
Basle Town	0	1	0	0	0	0	0	1
Basle Country	0	0	1	0	0	0	0	1
Schaffhausen	0	1	0	1	0	0	0	2
Appenzell-Outer Rhodes	0	1	0	0	0	0	0	1
Appenzell-Inner Rhodes	1	0	0	0	0	0	0	1
St. Gallen	1	1	0	0	0	0	0	2
Grisons	1	0	0	0	0	0	1	2
Aargau	1	1	0	0	0	0	0	2
Thurgau	0	1	0	1	0	0	0	2
Ticino	1	1	0	0	0	0	0	2
Vaud	0	1	0	0	0	1	0	2
Valais	2	0	0	0	0	0	0	2
Neuchâtel	0	1	0	0	0	1	0	2
Geneva	0	1	0	0	0	1	0	2
Total	18	13	3	4	0	3	3	44

Federal Assembly sessions. In contrast, on a local level, an individual can maintain his own occupation while contributing to the political life of his canton. Furthermore, elections to the federal legislature are essentially cantonal affairs. Not only is the canton the electoral district, but it is customary to limit election to those persons who have proved themselves in cantonal affairs, usually through participation in the legislatures.

The third and most salient reason for the cantonal nature of Swiss politics is the fact that there are no nation-wide elections that demand a national organization for their success. The seven members of the Federal Council, the Swiss executive, are chosen by the members of the Federal Assembly, who in turn have been elected on a cantonal basis. As Rappard has pointed out, the initiatives and referenda are no substitute for national elections. Usually they are not strictly party affairs and, furthermore, do not arouse the same fanatic partisan loyalties as the election of an American President, for example, who is also the head of his party.

Consequently, the parties whose history and principles we have investigated must be considered as loose confederations of independent cantonal parties. It is on the cantonal level that the fund-raising and the recruitment of members occur. Organization and even the names of the parties vary from canton to canton as does the degree of loyalty to the party principles espoused by the national platforms. So great are the differences, in fact, that often a voter must shift his party allegiance, when moving from one canton to another, in order to find a party with a compatible doctrine. It is also on the cantonal level that decisions are made to cooperate with other parties in elections. In the *Annuaire statistique* for 1953, to cite an instance, members of both the Radical and Farmers parties in the cantonal legislature of Turgovie are listed together under the Radical heading, with a notation that "in several electoral circles there was a common list." On the other hand, the delegates of the two parties to the Federal Assembly are listed separately.[4]

Nevertheless, in the course of time national party organizations have been created on these cantonal foundations. To a certain extent this evolution has reflected the increase in the importance of the federal government *vis-à-vis* the cantons. It also reflects the increasingly wide distribution of political party strength as well as the realization that weak local parties can sometimes be aided by bringing to bear the weight of a national organization. The functions of the national party organizations are mostly limited to discussion of major national issues, adopting party policy toward initiatives and referenda, drawing up party platforms, and in general engaging in propaganda. Decisions, however, are not considered binding upon the cantonal parties or the party's representatives in parliament, but rather recommendations for their general guidance. Even candidates for major public office, including those for the Federal Assembly, often tend to emphasize their personal records and cantonal issues rather than their national party platform.

Most parties have a three-level structure. At the base there is a fairly large conference composed mainly of delegates from cantonal parties whose main task it is once a year to adopt party platforms, elect the party president, and in general approve the decisions of other party organs. In the center there is a smaller organ, usually called the

[4] See pp. 507 and 508.

Central Committee, which meets more frequently and whose task it is to make more pressing decisions, draft party platforms for the approval of the lower body, and generally direct the affairs of the party. At the top there is an even smaller body, perhaps two dozen men, to effect the proper execution of the decisions of the more representative body, to attend to current affairs of the party, and to provide for leadership. Of special importance in every party is the full-time Secretary who, with a small staff, maintains a permanent headquarters in Berne. Organs to study specific areas of policy, or to propagandize and recruit among various sectors of society, are created as needed. All parties attempt to keep in close liaison with their representatives in parliament.[5]

A quick look at the structure of the Catholic Conservative party, for example, should provide us with a better idea of the actual organization of a Swiss party. In the first place, the Swiss Catholic Conservative party is composed of "cantonal parties which acknowledge its program (principles and political directives) and which pledge themselves to respect its statutes."[6] There is no attempt to impose any real degree of uniformity on the cantonal members since they remain "independent as concerns their cantonal politics, their internal organization, and their choice of a name."[7]

The three major organs of the Catholic Conservative party are the Assembly of Delegates, the Central Committee, and the Executive Committee. The Assembly of Delegates, which meets once a year, is composed of delegates from the member cantonal political parties (one for each thousand votes received in the most recent federal election), delegates from other organizations which cooperate with the party on doctrinal matters, members of the Catholic Conservative group in the federal parliament, members of the Central Committee, members of permanent study commissions, and representatives of the party press. The size of this body varies anywhere from three to five hundred. Its most important tasks are to elect the party's President and fifteen members of the Central Committee, to establish the party's official position on important federal referenda, to ratify the annual reports of the party and the parliamentary group, and to approve the party program and statutes on the basis of drafts submitted by the Central Committee. Additional meetings of the Assembly of Delegates may be

[5] There are, of course, variations in party structure. The Socialists, for instance, tend more toward autonomy than federalism and some of the minor parties have never found it expedient to create such a complex structure.

[6] *Statuts du Parti conservateur-chrétien-social suisse,* adopted in Lucerne on February 10, 1957, Art. 2.

[7] *Ibid.,* Art. 4.

called as the need arises. The party statutes also provide for the calling of a Party Congress, open to all legitimate party members (only those who are members of the Assembly of Delegates have the right to vote, however), "to mark the opening of the electoral campaign for the federal parliament or when the political situation or important events require a large party demonstration."[8]

The Central Committee, which meets twice a year, is composed of: (1) the presidents of the cantonal parties; (2) fifteen delegates from the parliamentary group; (3) fifteen members elected by the Assembly of Delegates; (4) twenty-one delegates from affiliated groups, such as the Association of Catholic Farmers; (5) presidents of the permanent study commissions; (6) five delegates from affiliated youth groups; (7) five delegates from the Association of Catholic Publicists; and (8) members of the Catholic press accredited to the Federal Assembly. This organ is of a more manageable size with a membership of around 100 persons. The major duties of the Central Committee are to elect the party's vice-presidents, elect the members of the Executive Committee, elect the presidents of the permanent study commissions, prepare draft platforms and statutes for presentation to the Assembly of Delegates, open campaigns for constitutional initiatives or legislative referenda, fix the party's official position on referenda when the Assembly has not been called for that purpose, and decide on the admission and exclusion of cantonal party organizations.

At the top of the organizational structure is found the Executive Committee made up of the President of the party, the Vice-Presidents, and from twelve to sixteen other members elected by the Central Committee.[9] The major purpose of this organ is to represent the party, execute the decisions of the Assembly of Delegates and the Central Committee, supervise the general activities of the party, and assure the party's liaison with the federal authorities, the parliamentary group, the cantonal parties, and the press. Specifically, it convokes meetings of the Assembly of Delegates and the Central Committee and prepares their agenda, elects the Secretary General, and an Assistant Secretary General for French-speaking Switzerland, adopts the budget, names the members of the permanent study commission, and elects the party's treasurer.[10]

Liaison with the party's representatives in the federal parliament

[8] *Ibid.*, Art. 20.

[9] In 1960 there were three vice-presidents and sixteen elected members which, with the party president, gave it a membership of twenty persons.

[10] There are nine permanent study commissions of from fifteen to thirty members reporting to the Executive Committee. The nine areas of study include: foreign affairs, national defense, cultural policies, finance, economics, agriculture, social policies, family, tourism, and transport.

is carried out through a number of devices. The parliamentary group "which acts on its own responsibility" sends a report of its activities each year to the Assembly of Delegates.[11] The Executive Committee and a committee of the parliamentary group must, as a rule, have a joint meeting once before or during each parliamentary session to examine current political problems. Further, all the members of parliament are members of the Assembly of Delegates, fifteen of their number are also members of the Central Committee, and the parliamentary group must be represented on all of the permanent study commissions. In practice, the parliamentary members provide for a great deal of the direction of the national party. In 1960, for example, fourteen out of the twenty members of the Executive Committee were deputies to the National Council and the Council of States.

The activities of the national Catholic Conservative party are financed by dues from cantonal parties and party members of parliament, and from annual "voluntary contributions."

Interest Groups

Interest group activity in Switzerland is integrated, to a very great extent, into the normal political process. One of the more important reasons for this is the multi-party system. Although there are no extreme differences in philosophy between the existing parties, the political platforms and activities of the party's representatives do reflect a divergence in attitude towards many of the major problems of the day — economic, social, and political. Interest groups therefore can usually find a party whose attitude reflects their chosen position and make common cause. If such a party should not exist, the nature of the Swiss system of proportional representation makes it relatively easy to start a new party with a favorable orientation. This is true on the cantonal level as well as on the national level.

The nature of the parliamentary system also is favorable to interest group activity. The lack of salaries for parliamentarians and the growing length of parliamentary sessions make it difficult for a professional politician to exist. Even the self-employed, who might be considered more independent, such as lawyers with private practices, are finding it more and more difficult to afford parliamentary service. Their places are being taken by trade and industrial union officials, and even by industrial executives, all of whose salaries are continued during tenure and for whom replacements are hired to carry out their normal duties.

[11] *Ibid.*, Art. 25. It should be recalled that Art. 91 of the federal Constitution provides that the members of the federal parliament must vote without instruction.

There is also the traditional abhorrence of the Swiss voter for the professional politician. When men are drafted for political office, their backgrounds of success in private life, business, farming, or labor union activity is usually the deciding issue.

Interest group activity is also possible at several stages of the legislative process. The Federal Council makes it a practice to call upon groups that might be affected by new legislation to state their views or even help draft the new law.[12] Testimony from interest groups is also called for by the legislative committees which give new legislation its first close scrutiny.

Interest groups can always turn to the legislative referendum. If the legislature should pass a law that a particular group found too distasteful, it can always attempt to force a legislative referendum. The tendency of the Swiss voters to reject a goodly portion of legislation when brought before them for the first time can be a powerful weapon. The constitutional initiative is also valuable. Although a constitutional initiative has even less chance of being accepted by the voters, the placing of an issue before all of the people can have tremendous publicity value for the cause of the interest group.

Four of the most powerful Swiss interest groups are the Swiss Union of Commerce and Industry (*Schweizerische Handels- und Industrie-Verein*), commonly called the VORORT; the Swiss Peasants Union (*Schweizersche Bauernverband*); the Swiss Federation of Trade Unions (*Schweizerische Gewerkschaftsbund*); and the Swiss Association of Arts and Crafts (*Schweizerische Gewerbeverband*). The VORORT is an association of interest groups in specialized fields of industry and commerce such as the powerful Swiss Society of Machinery Manufacturers and the Swiss Watch Chamber. The Farmers Union, in a like manner, is an association of specialized interest groups in the field of agriculture and meat producers such as the Winegrowers Association of Western Switzerland, the Swiss Brown Cattle Race Association, the Swiss Association of Producers of Cattle for Slaughter, and the Association of Swiss Master Butchers. The Swiss Federation of Trade Unions brings together trade unions in various fields such as the Swiss Railway Employers Union, the Swiss Federation of Construction and Wood Workers, the Swiss Federation of Metal and Watch Workers, and the Swiss Federation of Workers in Commerce, Transportation, and Food Industries. The Swiss Association of Arts and Crafts, often dubbed the "small business association of Switzerland," is organized in a similar manner by small business groups.

[12] Paragraph 3 of article 32 of the Constitution provides for consultation between the Federal Council and the interested groups.

All four major interest groups are usually represented in the Federal Assembly. In 1958, for example, four National Councillors and one Councillor of State were officials of the Swiss Peasants Union or its affiliates including the president of the union and a member of its executive committee. In the same year the Swiss Association of Arts and Crafts had its president, vice-president, and honorary president all in the National Council. The Swiss Federation of Trade Unions was represented by fifteen National Councillors and the VORORT by several industrialists or senior officers of firms associated with it. There are many more private interest groups in Switzerland which whether or not represented in parliament, can always bring their weight to bear in favor of or against legislation that touches upon their interests. Of those with interests similar to the big four, one should not fail to take into account the Union of Swiss Chambers of Commerce Abroad, the Catholic-sponsored trade unions, and the several employers' associations. Groups whose· interests are further afield are many. For examples of the variety that exists, one could mention the feminist movements, such specialized groups as the Swiss alpinist guide associations, and the Swiss automobile associations.

Some criticism of the existing interest group system has been voiced, but the proponents are nevertheless still in a majority. Some argue that all interests must be permitted their say in order to make it possible to determine what is the national interest. Others have faith that the manner of selecting the legislative members, and the manner of selection and composition of the collegiate Federal Council, including the latter's important place in the legislative mechanics, will insure that the Swiss public servant will remain true to his political, legal, and moral responsibilities. If worst comes to worst, the Swiss voter has confidence in his own ability to choose right from wrong. After all, the majority still has its ultimate weapon, the referendum, backed by the constitutional initiative.

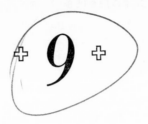

Domestic Policies

One of the more striking facets of government in Switzerland over the past one hundred years is the increasing scope of activities in which the federal authorities engage. As in other countries that have experienced the same tendency, it has been due to numerous causes. The concentration and centralization of economic power and the increasing dependence of Swiss prosperity on international trade have resulted in calls for national intervention. Government controls have been brought about by the inability of the economy to regulate itself in times of stress, as for example in the depression of the 1930's. Switzerland has not escaped the results of the gradual change in the individual's concept of the duty of the State from that of protector of liberty to that of a guarantor of the minimum conditions necessary to the good life. Finally, although Switzerland has not been involved in a foreign war for over a century, it has been faced repeatedly with the need to mobilize to defend its frontiers. As the student of government is well aware, controls necessary for the mobilization of national resources in times of international tension often are difficult to eliminate in times of peace.

This chapter will be devoted to an investigation of the scope of the activities of the Swiss federal government in the domestic sector, rather than to the degree of federal control as contrasted to local control that was discussed earlier under the rubric of federalism. It will include government monopolies, government economic activities, and government responsibility for social welfare. The Swiss military system will be considered also, and the problem of financing the government's activities.

State Monopolies

The Swiss federal government has been granted a virtual monopoly in certain areas of the economy. From the point of view of policy, some of the more interesting ones that will be discussed here are the gunpowder and alcohol monopoly, the bank note monopoly and the Swiss National Bank, the government-operated communications system, and the Swiss federal railways.

The oldest in Swiss experience is the gunpowder monopoly granted to the federation in the Constitution of 1848. The manufacture of gunpowder and its sale are reserved exclusively to the Confederation. Mining explosives and dynamite are exempted. The principal factories are located in Worblaufen (Berne), Thoune, and Altdorf, and the principal powder magazines are located in Lucerne and Berne. A series of amendments to the original article have extended the monopoly over almost all materials of war and have granted the federal government the sole power over their manufacture, sale, importation, and exportation. Although a minimal profit has accrued to the state from this monopoly, its purpose was primarily for public security. A constitutional amendment accepted by the people on November 24, 1957, has extended federal control to atomic energy.

Disturbance over what was considered to be an abuse of the use of intoxicating spirits led to the approval, in 1885, of a constitutional amendment to permit the federal government to legislate on the manufacture and sale of distilled liquors and industrial alcohol. A government alcohol monopoly was created by legislation, approved in a referendum, which came into effect in May, 1887. As a result of further modification in 1930, 1932, and 1945, the government gained almost complete control over all beverages with high alcoholic content. The government may either manufacture alcohol itself or may license private enterprises. Private distillation has come under government control as have the import and export of all liquors. The alcohol monopoly is directed by the Federal Alcohol Administration and supervised by the legislature. Half of the net receipts from the alcohol monopoly are kept by the Confederation for old age and survivors' insurance; and half are turned over to the cantons, 10 per cent of which must be set aside to combat alcoholism.[1] It is interesting to note that Article 32 *ter* of the Constitution prohibits the manufacture, importation, transport, and sale of absinthe except for "pharmaceutical purposes."

After several unsuccessful attempts, in 1891 the Swiss government persuaded the people to accept a constitutional amendment granting the federal authorities a bank note monopoly. Legislation to create a

[1] For a discussion of Swiss legislation on alcohol see Dr. V. J. Steiger, *Développement, principes et application de la législation sur l'alcool en Suisse, La Question de l'alcool en Suisse, Cahier 25* (Basle, 1954).

bank for the issue and control of bank notes, however, was not approved by the people until 1905 — and then only after the legislators left open the questions of where the bank was to be located and whether it was to be private or a state bank. The bank opened its doors finally in 1907. As the legislation now stands (an additional constitutional amendment was approved in 1951), the Swiss National Bank is a private bank under the direct supervision and control of the federal authorities with its administrative seat in Berne and its directorial seat in Zurich. The federal government has the right, on one year's notice, to nationalize the bank. Along with its authority over bank notes, the Swiss National Bank now is responsible for stabilizing the Swiss money market, facilitating payments, and in general following a credit and monetary policy best fitted to serve the general interests of the country.

After payment of interest or "reasonable dividends" to shareholders and deductions of payments to a reserve fund, two-thirds of the net profits of the bank are turned over to the cantons. The bank and its branches are exempt from all cantonal taxation.

The transport of mail has been a federal monopoly in Switzerland since 1848 and the telegraph service since the constitutional revision of 1874. Subsequent legislation has expanded these monopolies to include telephone, radio, and television. Under the overall direction of the executive Department of Posts and Railroads, there is a director of posts, a director of telegraphs, and a director of telephones. While the facilities for radio and television are under the control of the Department of Posts and Railroads, Switzerland has turned programming over to the *Société Suisse de Radiodiffusion,* an amalgamation of non-profit-making regional broadcasting organizations.

The largest economic enteprise over which the federal government exercises complete control is the Swiss railway system. During the first fifty years of Swiss federal history, railroads were in private hands with the cantons exercising powers of control. The federal government's role was confined to establishing rules for the standardization of equipment on the various lines and for the use of trains for the transport of the mail and military equipment. As the number of railroads grew, it was found that there were increasing conflicts of authority between cantons. In order to eliminate the conflicts and to standardize railroad regulation, the federal government made itself the sole regulating agency in 1872. In addition to passing a standard railroad law, it established a railway pension and savings fund and regulated the hours of work of the operating employees. Finally, in 1898, with overwhelming popular approval, it nationalized all of the principal railways. The reasons given for the move included the need to provide service for areas which would be unprofitable for private enterprise and the desire to eliminate control of foreign stockholders who were in a majority in a few of the major lines.[2]

At present the Swiss Federal Railway is an autonomous governmental corporation obliged to carry out its work on a businesslike basis and is protected from political influence. Heading the railways is a policy-making administrative council of fifteen members appointed by the Federal Council and a three-man directorate in charge of operations. Its seat is in Berne. There are three administrative subdivisions with headquarters located in Lausanne, Lucerne, and Zurich, each of which is under the control of a district director. The finances of the railway system are handled separately from those of the Confederation, although the Confederation guarantees its debt. In 1935 and 1946 the people rejected proposals that would have given the government power to regulate the division of traffic between trains and trucks and to limit competition between trucks and the federal railway.

Commerce and Industry

The involvement of the Swiss federal government in commerce and industry, with the exception of some of the instances mentioned above, is essentially a twentieth-century phenomenon. Few powers were granted in the 1848 Constitution, and in 1874 a provision was added guaranteeing "the freedom of trade and commerce."[3] The real impetus came with the depression of the 1930's, reinforced in the 1940's by World War II. In an effort to overcome the effects of the depression, the government began regulating the marketing of goods, placing restrictions on credit and currency transactions, and granting loans and subsidies to certain particularly affected sectors of the economy. Government control of commerce and industry was increased during World War II. Much of the action taken was unconstitutional, or at least extra-constitutional, relying upon broad emergency legislation or the power to make urgent *arrêtes*.

In 1947, by a series of amendments to the Constitution, most of the government's emergency powers over commerce and industry were sanctioned for regular future use. Article 31 *bis,* one of the more important constitutional changes, illustrates well the range of control the Confederation can now legally employ. It provides that the Confederation may take any "measures necessary for the general welfare and economic security of its citizens." With due regard for the general

[2] For a discussion of the Swiss railway system before expropriation, see Brooks, *Government and Politics of Switzerland,* pp. 204–224.

[3] Art. 31.

interests of the national economy, "the Confederation may regulate commerce and industry and take measures in favor of particular branches of the economy or professions." "If justified in the national interest," the Confederation may deviate from the principle of "freedom of commerce and industry," and undertake measures necessary to (1) preserve important branches of the economy or professions whose existence is in jeopardy; (2) maintain a healthy and productive agriculture and a strong agricultural population; (3) protect distressed areas; (4) prevent harmful economic and social effects of cartels and similar groups; and (5) insure preparedness in case of war.

There are two excellent examples of the use to which the powers of the Swiss federal government can be put, in watchmaking and in agriculture. One of the early uses of the 1947 "economic articles" was the passage of a federal law in 1951 concerning the watchmaking industry, which had begun to suffer from foreign competition as early as the 1920's. Most severely hit were the many small firms whose production represented a large portion of the total manufacture of Swiss watches. Through industry-wide agreements and legislation under federal emergency powers, an attempt was made to preserve a fair share of the market for these small enterprises. The law of 1951 codified these measures on a constitutional basis. The export of watchmaking machinery was placed under federal license and government permission was required for the opening of any new Swiss watch factories or the increase of the number of workers in any existing ones. The government was authorized also to create a crisis fund based on contributions from the watch industry. This fund is under the control of the government and can be used at its discretion to encourage scientific research or to help workers affected by any economic crisis in the industry.[4] The 1951 law was revised in 1961 to permit the government also to control the quality of watches produced in Switzerland and to prohibit the sale of substandard items.[5]

Of all the areas of the Swiss economy, the hand of government has fallen most heavily on agriculture. Under the authority of the so-called "economic articles" introduced in 1947, the government has passed two important laws, one concerning the maintenance of rural land-owning and one dealing with the "improvement of agriculture and the maintenance of the peasant population." The former sets strict rules as to the disposal of farm property. Preference must be granted to relatives of the seller and his employees. Farm land must not be sold for speculative purposes or for nonfarm purposes without authorization by the

[4] See Sauser-Hall, *Guide politique suisse,* p. 243.
[5] See *Statut légal de l'horlogerie du 23 juin 1961.*

state. A minimum time limit is set between the date of purchase and of subsequent sale of farm land. The second law, promulgated in 1951, came into effect in progressive stages in 1954 and 1955. This law deals with almost every aspect of the agricultural economy. The government may take the measures necessary to ensure that a minimum of Swiss land is retained in production, to encourage agricultural pursuits, and to encourage the growth of crops considered vital. The government has the power to limit the imports of certain agricultural crops or to raise the import duties or to force the importers to dispose of a certain portion of Swiss crops. The government also can take other measures necessary, including stockpiling, to keep the prices of crops at a desirable level. Complementary laws promulgated in 1953 and 1954 broadened the government's responsibility to include wine, meat, milk, and eggs. To this should be added the responsibility to ensure the country a permanent reserve of cereals. The constitutional amendment in question specifies that a minimum reserve of 80,000 tons of food grains must be maintained at all times.[6]

To a certain extent the government's agricultural policies may stem from a desire on the part of some to encourage government economic planning for planning's sake and from the political power of the agricultural population. But there is no doubt that they stem also from a desire to keep Switzerland as self-sufficient as possible with regard to food in the event of future European or world conflicts.

Social Legislation

The Swiss have a fairly comprehensive system of social legislation. The three most important pieces of social legislation are the Factory Act of 1877, the Sickness and Accident Insurance Act of 1911, and the Old Age and Survivors Insurance Act of 1946.

Between 1848 and 1877 the enactment of laws on labor standards was a cantonal affair. Several of the more progressive cantons were attempting labor legislation as early as the 1850's, but there was a great divergence among cantonal standards. Article 34 of the constitutional revision of 1874 placed the matter in the hands of the Confederation. The Factory Act of 1877 was the first excursion by the federal authorities into the field. Revised in 1914 and in 1919 and supplemented by laws such as the Federal Law on the Minimum Age of Workers and the Federal Law on Home Work of 1940, and the Law on Weekly Rest of 1931, the Swiss have evolved a fairly advanced national labor code.

A few examples should suffice to give an idea of present-day labor

[6] Sauser-Hall, *Guide* . . .. pp. 149–50 and 243–246.

controls. Since 1919 the work week in factories in Switzerland has been fixed at forty-eight hours. However, the Federal Council may permit an extension of the work week to fifty-two hours or more in certain industries if a shorter work week would place that industry in a disadvantageous position in foreign competition. All workers must be given a one-hour lunch period in the middle of the day, or two half-hour periods. In principle, night work and Sunday work are forbidden. Night work under Swiss law is any work from 8.00 P.M. to 5:00 A.M. in the summer, and to 6:00 A.M. in the winter. Those industries the nature of which demand continuous operation must obtain a special permit from the Federal Council and must follow specified rules. No one may be forced to work at night, for instance, and all employees of such industries must receive one day of rest per week. That day of rest must be a Sunday at least every other week. A law of 1931 extends this rule to employees in commerce, artisans, hotel employees, and others in similar occupations.

There are particular rules pertaining to women and children. Women may not be employed in night work and may not be permitted to work on Sundays. Pregnant women must stop work at least six weeks before the anticipated date of delivery. Children under fifteen years of age may not be employed in factories. Children between fifteen and eighteen may not work nights or Sundays, and all children up to the age of eighteen must be given five hours or more a week free to attend classes.[7]

Inspection of working conditions in factories is carried out by a staff of federal inspectors working under the control of the Federal Council. A Factory Commission, made up of an equal number of representatives of management and labor, advises the Federal Council on all labor problems of a general nature. As a general rule, labor relations have not been the cause of much trouble since the general strike of 1918. In 1962, for example, only 1,386 working days were lost in all of Switzerland as a result of strikes. The federal government has not, therefore, been under too much pressure to legislate in this field.[8]

As a result of the broad powers over the economy placed in the hands of the Confederation by the 1947 amendments to the Constitution, it can be expected that the federal authorities will propose a new labor and industry code in the near future. This new code will un-

---

[7] See Sauser-Hall, *Guide . . .,* pp. 240–242.

[8] For a discussion of the Swiss compromise between closed shops and union shops, and a general view of Swiss labor relations, see Michael Dudra, "The Swiss System of Union Security," *Labor Law Journal,* X (March, 1959), 165–174.

doubtedly contain stricter rules for work in industry and will extend federal protection for work in other occupations not now as completely covered as industry. Several groups that will be affected by the new code are already making their desires known. The Swiss trade union oganization, for instance, has deposited a petition signed by some 123,000 voters for a constitutional initiative to introduce the forty-four hour week in Switzerland. The group has left no doubt that the purpose of the initiative is to put pressure on the Federal Council.[9]

The Sickness and Accident Insurance Act of 1911 provides for a combination compulsory and voluntary accident insurance plan and a voluntary sickness insurance plan. An attempt to introduce a completely compulsory accident and sickness insurance plan was turned down in a referendum in 1900. The accident insurance plan introduced in 1911 is managed by a Federal Accident Insurance Fund with its base of operation in Lucerne. The Fund operates as an autonomous federal monopoly although it remains under the supervision of the Confederation and receives generous federal subsidies. Accident insurance is compulsory for the employees of all federal monopolies and for private enterprises of a certain size whose work is especially dangerous. Premiums for insurance against accidents at work are paid by the employer. If a person wishes to be insured against other accidents he must pay the added premium himself. In case of accident, the Fund pays for doctors' bills and medicines and awards the injured a percentage of his normal salary. In case of death from an accident, the Fund pays for the funeral and awards the surviving members of the employee's family annual payments equal to 60 per cent of the normal salary of the deceased. Almost any Swiss for whom the accident insurance is not compulsory may join the plan.

Insurance against sickness is the responsibility of non-profit insurance agencies and is completely voluntary. The Act of 1911 permits the Confederation to subsidize such agencies up to a fixed amount. Agencies which received federal subsidies, however, must have their base of operations in Switzerland and must submit their regulations for federal approval. Yearly financial reports also must be submitted to the Federal Council.

[9] See the *Journal de Genève* (April 12, 1960), 2. A similar initiative proposed by the Duttweiler Independent Party was rejected in a referendum on October 26, 1958. It was generally agreed that the rejection was due not to the nature of the initiative but the group which had initiated it. The forty-four hour work week has already been introduced into several sectors of the economy, including federal employees and employees in the chemical industry.

The most important recent action in the field of social legislation is the Old Age and Survivors Insurance Act of 1946, approved in referendum on July 6, 1947. This Act, which came into effect on January 1, 1948, and has been amended several times, provides for compulsory insurance for all residents of Switzerland. Even Swiss living in foreign countries are permitted to become members of the plan. Contributions are made from the age of twenty to the age of sixty-five. In exceptional cases they may begin at the age of fifteen for those who are gainfully employed. Wage earners and salaried employees contribute 2 per cent of their earnings, which is matched by the employer. Self-employed persons pay 4 per cent. Both the cantons and the federal government contribute toward the expenses of the plan. Payments begin at the age of 65 and the amount received depends upon the annual salary of the insured. A single wage earner who reaches the age of 65 receives from between 720 to 1,700 Swiss francs a year, a married couple from 1,160 to 2,720 francs. Payments to widows depends upon their age and the length of time they were married, with a minimum of 580 francs a year. A child who has lost one parent receives from 220 to 510 francs a year up to the age of eighteen, or twenty if the child is still in school or working as an apprentice. A child who has lost both parents receives from 350 to 765 francs a year.[10]

It should be noted also that Article 34 *quinquies* of the Swiss Constitution, approved in referendum on November 20, 1945, gives the federal government the power to legislate on family insurance funds, to institute compulsory maternity insurance, and to finance public housing.

The Army

The Swiss army has two primary missions: (1) to deter any potential enemy from invading Swiss territory; and (2) to defend the integrity and independence of the Swiss state if an attack should nevertheless occur. Because no country has dared to attack Switzerland since the federal system was introduced in 1848, it can be deduced that the first mission has successfully been carried out. By the same token, it is impossible to tell whether the Swiss army has been strong enough to undertake its second mission. The military system that has been evolved to carry out these purposes is based on two principles: (1) defense is primarily a national affair, although responsibility in some instances is shared between the Confederation and the cantons; and (2), military force shall be in the form of a militia rather than a professional army.

[10] See Sauser-Hall, *Guide* . . . , pp. 204–211. Increased by 30% in 1961.

Under the Constitution of 1848, the army was almost completely in the hands of the cantons in time of peace, with some joint control in time of war. The weakness of such a system became evident during the Franco-Prussian War of 1870–71 when the army was mobilized for fear of a violation of Swiss territory by one of the belligerents. The constitutional revision of 1874 considerably strengthened the hand of the federal government. Federal laws enacted periodically under the new constitutional provisions have continued the process of centralization.

At present the Confederation is responsible for the overall organization of the Swiss army, its command in both peacetime and wartime, and its supervision. To the cantons are left the tasks of enforcing military regulations and providing some of the personal equipment of the troops. The Confederation also permits the cantons to organize a few infantry and reserve units and to appoint the officers for these units up to and including the rank of lieutenant-colonel. The Confederation organizes all other units, including the auxiliary services such as military aviation, and appoints all other officers.

In peacetime the head of the Swiss army is the Federal Councillor in charge of the Military Department. He has at his disposal the general staff and experts in all branches of the service. There are no officers above the rank of colonel in peacetime. If general mobilization should occur, the Federal Assembly appoints a Commander in Chief who assumes direction of the army. His appointment lapses at the end of the emergency. Only four commanders in chief have been elected since 1848, General Doufour in 1849 and again in 1856, General Herzog in 1870, General Wille in 1914, and General Guisan in 1939.[11]

Traditionally, Switzerland's military strength has been founded on two important elements, it geography and its manpower. The mountainous character of most of its frontiers was considered a natural barrier to the movement of enemy troops, with reinforcements where necessary in the form of underground fortifications and gun emplacements. Areas where the topography did not provide for natural protection were to be defended by fortifications and large numbers of infantry with supporting artillery. Above all, the objective of the defenses of Switzerland was to provide such a strength at the frontiers as to discourage the enemy or if necessary to deny even a single foothold on Swiss soil.

[11] For a discussion of the relationship between the Federal Councillor in charge of the Military Department and the Commander in Chief in times of emergency, see Hughes, *The Federal Constitution of Switzerland,* pp. 17–18.

To provide the large number of troops necessary to defend the frontiers, emphasis was placed on having as large as possible a civilian army ready for any emergency. Universal military training has almost always been the rule. Article 18 of the Constitution of 1848, carried over into the Constitution of 1874, provides that: "All Swiss are liable to military service." It is customary in Switzerland for all young men who have attained the age of twenty to be called to the colors and put through a basic training course, then to be recalled at stated intervals to receive refresher courses. The number of refresher courses that the Swiss male must undergo decreases with his age. Soldiers in special services, such as the cavalry, and officers and non-commissioned officers undergo additional training or attend special schools as necessary. In 1960, for instance, the Swiss male retained his army affiliation until the age of sixty. From 20 to 36 years of age he was considered part of the Elite, from 37 to 48 a part of the Landwehr, and from 49 to 60 a part of the Landsturm. The amount of additional training, after the basic training course, and the tasks to which the three classes were assigned varied according to the age group included.

In order to insure that military service would not become too great a burden on the individual, a system of social security was initiated. The Confederation insures all military personnel against sickness and accident. The payment to the sick or injured may reach 80 to 90 per cent of their normal salary. Further, if a family of a serviceman is likely to become destitute as a result of the calling up of the head of the family the commune of residence must provide relief. The expense is borne by the Confederation and the canton in a three-to-one ratio. During the period 1939 to 1945, the federal government created a compensation fund to cover the major part of loss of income by soldiers called to the colors.

In principle no one is exempt from military service. Exceptions, of course, are made for those unable to serve, such as those physically and mentally unfit and those whose services are too essential to permit them to take the necessary time off from their civilian occupations. Among the latter are members of the Federal Council, the Chancellor of the Confederation, members of the clergy who do not become military chaplains, and directors and wardens of prisons. All such individuals are exempt during their tenure in office. Other groups considered essential to the defense effort, such as customs officials, police, and indispensable employees of transportation enterprises, are exempt after completing a course in the school for recruits. Other exemptions from military service are rare, but if obtained make the person liable to the special military exemption tax based on both income and capital, which must be paid annually. All Swiss who reside outside Switzerland must also pay the annual military exemption tax.

The actual organization of the army and the composition of its units are determined by the competent federal authorities on the basis of the needs of the times. The lessons of World War II, for instance, accounted for at least two reorganizations. The equipment of the soldiers was brought up to date, fire power and mobility were increased, and air defenses and communications were improved. Nevertheless, most of the reorganizations of the army were based on the concept of static defense, or at least upon the principle that the primary purpose of the army was to prevent any potential enemy from setting foot on Swiss territory. Mobile reserves were to be used to back up defensive positions or to be moved into areas where an enemy might break through the first line of defense. An infantry army clinging stubbornly to every inch of Swiss territory was the basic rule.

The reorganization plans unveiled by the Federal Council in July, 1960, represented a major breakthrough from the older concept of defense.[12] The purpose of the new plan was to replace static defense with mobility. The accent on mobility stemmed from the fear that the old defensive establishment could not meet the needs of new methods of warfare developed since World War II, especially "tactical" atomic weapons. Only a high degree of mobility would permit the dispersion of troops necessary to avoid a disastrous loss of effectives in case of an atomic bombardment, and at the same time permit the army to concentrate its forces in sufficient strength to cut off and destroy enemy salients and if necessary carry the fight rapidly to enemy bases. The increasing development of use of airborne troops was another strong reason for the increase in mobility of Swiss troops. Another reason for reorganization for mobility — one that was understood, but which was not emphasized particularly — was to provide for a military organization capable of using its own "tactical" weapons in the future.

To meet these new needs, the Federal Council proposed a variety of changes in the organization of the army, including a reorganization of military units to provide for better coordination, the creation of special mobilized divisions to be deployed in the vulnerable plateau area, increased mechanization of transport, increased fire power for all units, and a slight decrease in the number of older military personnel. Among the specifics of the reorganization plan were the drastic reduction in the number of independent infantry battalions, the elimination of the horse cavalry, a reduction in the number

[12] For the texts of the proposal and the accompanying message, see *Feuille fédérale*, 1960, II, pp. 321–412.

of aircraft from 400 to 300, and the creation of three special mobile divisions for deployment in the plateau area. (Before submission of its plans to the Federal Assembly, the Federal Council had considered the creation of six such divisions; the number was decreased from six to three because of the expense that would be involved.) The Federal Council also proposed the lowering of the age limits of servicemen. The Elite would be composed of men from 20 to 32, the Landwehr from 33 to 42, and the Landstrum from 43 to 50. Men over 50 and officers over 55 would in principle be released. These changes, according to the Federal Council, would not only ensure that the army would be made up of those physically able to stand the strenuous activity of modern military life, but also would release more people for activity in the proposed new civil defense organization and for civilian occupations essential for the defensive effort. The change would also bring about substantial economies, as would the reduction in number of military aircraft.

Opposition to the plans of the Federal Council was immediately forthcoming and undertook various guises. The Socialists took issue with a statement by the Federal Council that Switzerland must have an army that could cooperate with an ally in the case of aggression. To the Socialists this was "a serious deviation from the traditional meaning of Swiss neutrality."[13] The answer, as one critic of the Socialists' position put it, was that "if the neutral nation itself is the victim of an attack — and neutral Switzerland cannot conceive of any other reason for becoming involved — all obligations imposed by the status of neutrality are of course automatically cancelled and the attacked country is free to decide whether it wishes to ask for military assistance or other kinds of support and from whom."[14] Of a more effective nature was the attack by the traditionalists led by two high-ranking officers, Colonel Max Weibel, Chief of Infantry, and Colonel Alfred Ernst, Commander of the 8th Infantry Division. In general, this group wished to retain the organization of the army as it has been established previously. It attacked the concept of mechanized mobility, arguing that only an infantry-oriented army could guarantee continued resistance in an atomic war. Specifically, it advocated that the Swiss maintain all existing divisions and independent infantry battalions, and that they create small armored brigades to work in support of infantry divisions rather than establish new mechanized divisions. The only major point on which they were willing to concede were the reduction of the air

[13] See Ernst Bieri, "Army Reform in Switzerland," *Swiss Review of World Affairs,* X (November, 1960), 1.
[14] *Ibid.*

force and the lowering of the age limit for obligatory military service from 60 to 50. Also extremely vocal, and as it turned out effective, were pressures from the horse cavalry to preserve its branch of the service.[15]

After several months of, for the Swiss, quite heated debate, the Federal Assembly approved most of the innovations proposed by the Federal Council. On two points, however, the traditionalists were victorious. First, all independent infantry battalions were maintained. Second, instead of eliminating the service as originally proposed, eighteen out of the existing twenty-four cavalry squadrons were retained. It was also decided to maintain the air force at a strength of 400 aircraft until 1964, at which time its status will be reviewed.

One thing is certain: the reorganization of the Swiss army will not end with the 1960 legislation. Further attempts on the part of the Federal Council to keep it abreast of modern conditions can be expected.

In concluding the discussion of the Swiss army system, another important point should be raised. Modern methods of warfare are bringing about another change in Swiss military philosophy, perhaps not so dramatic as that of "mobility" vs. "static defense," but just as fundamental. Although Article 13 of the Constitution expressly forbids the Confederation to maintain a standing army, the exceptions to this rule have been growing year by year. All commanders of divisions and corps now owe their entire time to the military. The federal government has increased its permanent troops by the establishment of an aviation corps and a unit occupied with the upkeep of military installations. The number of career instructors has increased tremendously as new military techniques have evolved. In order to keep practice in accord with the Constitution, an amendment may be necessary before long.

[15] It is interesting to note that the abolition of the horse cavalry was expected to have a profound effect on Swiss agriculture. Cavalry horses are purchased by the Confederation or furnished by the soldier. If purchased by the soldier, the Confederation reimburses the soldier half the price of the horse. If purchased by the Confederation, the soldier reimburses the Confederation half the price. In both cases the horse remains under the upkeep of the soldier and after ten full years, the soldier becomes the owner. In between training periods many of the horses are used for various tasks on the farm. The abolition of the federal subsidy for horses, if the new plan came into effect, was expected to result in a change-over on many farms from horse power to tractor power. For a further discussion of the contemplated effects of the change in the Swiss army, see *Journal de Genève* (April 7, 1960), 1–2, (July 14, 1960), 2; and *Gazette de Lausanne* (December 22, 1959), 1.

Financing the Government

Switzerland has not escaped the worldwide phenomenon of a steady increase in the cost of government and the concomitant problem of finding the revenue to pay for it. Because of the nature of the Swiss political system, the problem of finding revenue is as complicated there as it is anywhere in the world.

Prior to World War I the expense of government was relatively low, and usually income was sufficient to cover expenses. World War I, however, marked a change in Swiss finances. From 1914 to 1921 expenditures outran income by over 100 million francs a year. Although it was again possible to balance the budget in the period from 1922 to 1935, the expenses of running the government did not fall back to the pre-World War I level. The Second World War necessitated increased expenditures. A peak of 2,593,952,000 francs in total expenditures was reached in 1944. In the same year revenues brought in only 1,597,617,000, to leave a deficit of 996,335,000 francs. In the postwar period revenues once again have caught up with expenses, but, as was true after World War I, the level of expenses has remained high. A picture of the overall development of the Swiss financial situation is provided in Table 15.

Table 16 provides a general picture of the manner in which national public funds are expended in a fairly average year.[16]

The problem of raising revenue to cover the ever-increasing expenses of government has always been a concern to the Swiss. The federal government was given four major sources of revenue in the Constiution of 1848: (1) customs duties; (2) post office revenue; (3) revenue from the gunpowder monopoly; and (4) contributions from cantons. The constitutional revision of 1874 added one-half of the gross receipts from a tax on exemptions from military duty levied by the cantons and revenues from the telegraph monopoly.[17] Not only was direct taxation reserved to the cantons, but the Confederation was placed in a position of having to call on the cantons for help if it should not be able to meet expenses under its own taxing power.

Until World War I, the constitutional revenue powers were adequate to meet most of the needs of the Confederation. Customs duties turned

[16] *Annuaire statistique, 1957*, p. 419.

[17] The 1848 Constitution also had a provison permitting the Confederation to use the interest from a special war fund to be contributed by the cantons (Art. 40). This provision was deleted in 1874 and replaced by one granting the federal government the use of revenue from federal property (Art. 42, para. 1). Neither provided a great deal of revenue for the federal government.

Table 15

Swiss Finances
(in millions of francs)

Year	Ordinary Expenses	Ordinary Revenue	Total Consolidated Debt (excluding Federal Railroads)
1849/50*	3.7	4.1	4.1
1856/60*	7.5	7.9	7.4
1870	18.2	9.2	13.7
1880	21.7	23.1	35.0
1890	38.2	39.1	54.1
1900	60.2	58.5	68.4
1910	90.9	96.4	117.1
1920	616.3	439.3	1,605.9
1930	483.4	634.7	1,883.3
1940	1,806.8	932.9	2,962.9
1950	1,637.0	1,973.7	7,746.6
1960	2,601.1	3,316.1	5,935.1
1961	3,267.1	3,406.0	5,727.0
1962	3,684.2	4,116.6	5,468.6

* Annual average

Annuaire statistique, 1959/1960, p. 427, and *1963,* p. 423.

Table 16

Federal Expenses in 1962

Purpose	Amount (in Swiss francs)
Interest on debt	208,204,000
Higher government officials	5,412,000
Personnel	413,876,000
General expenses	911,795,000
Cantonal share of certain income	231,955,000
Social work (federal)	198,709,000
Federal subsidies	757,298,000
Land and buildings	825,582,000
Loans and grants	131,363,000

out to be the most profitable source of income, at times meeting up to 80 per cent of the annual budget. So successful was the Confederation in raising money that it began granting subsidies to the cantons after the cantons ceased making contributions in 1849. In 1913 subsidies to cantons took up about 25 per cent of the Confederation's annual revenue.

World War I struck two blows at the Confederation's revenue structure. Expenditures to provide for the nation's defense rose far beyond the normal income, and at the same time there was a drastic decrease in customs duties. To meet its obligations the federal government was forced to adopt a variety of measures. Loans were floated, and bank note circulation was increased. Using its 1914 grant of "full powers," the Federal Council imposed a tax on war profits. In 1915 the voters approved a special "war tax," the first direct tax ever levied by the federal government, to raise money for the mobilization of Swiss troops. Although it was intended to be a "single-shot" affair, it was re-introduced from 1919 to 1932 to liquidate the Confederation's war debts. The only permanent increase in the Confederation's revenue power resulting from actions taken during the war was a sales tax on commercial transactions. This new tax was added to its constitutional powers in 1917 with the provision that one-fifth of the revenue gained would be paid over to the cantons.

The Confederation picked up two new sources of income in the 1920's, a tax on tobacco and a portion of the receipts from a tax on distilled spirits. Revenue obtained from these taxes was intended to be used to help finance old age and sickness insurance, but since the original insurance plans were turned down by the voters, for a long time it was available for the general use of the Confederation.

Just about the time that the financial situation had become stable, when income was equalling outgo, Switzerland began to feel the effects of the great depression. In order to meet its new obligations, the Federal Assembly passed an "urgent" *arrêté* in 1933 permitting the federal government to levy a direct federal tax — a "crisis offering" — and giving it various indirect taxing powers. Among the latter was a tax on beer. In 1938 the voters and the cantons approved the Assembly's action but specified that it should come to an end by 1942.

Events in Europe in the late 1930's and the outbreak of World War II again threw Swiss federal finances into confusion. Large sums of money were needed immediately to prepare for the defense of Swiss frontiers, and later for mobilization of the army. In the first stage, the Confederation turned to the people. In June, 1939, the government was granted power to introduce a limited sales tax. Events began to move too quickly to await ordinary constitutional procedures, however. On August 30, 1939, the Federal Council was given full emergency powers which permitted almost any measure necessary to raise revenue. Almost immediately the Federal Council extended all the financial measures that had been initiated during the depression, and began looking for new sources of income. Two new indirect taxes were introduced, a luxury tax and a "compensation tax." The Federal Council also introduced new direct taxes. By the end of the war it had imposed: (1) a war profits tax; (2) a national defense tax; (3) a national defense "sacrifice" tax; (4) a withholding tax; and (5) a national defense contribution tax imposed on persons leaving Switzerland. The Federal Council also had recourse to several emergency loans.

For many obvious reasons, the cost of government did not decrease immediately after World War II. After a plan to reorganize federal finances on a sound basis was turned down in a referendum, the federal government continued for a while to enforce the wartime measures by decree. In 1950 permission was granted by the voters to continue wartime sources of income until 1954 while a search for an acceptable plan went on. Again in 1954 the government's plans were turned down, and again the people gave permission to continue most of the wartime measures.

Finally, in 1958, the federal government persuaded the people to accept a new plan for federal financing. But the new plan was a compromise. The only important permanent source of income given to the Confederation was the wartime withholding tax on revenue from liquid assets, lottery winnings, and certain gains from insurance. All other changes in the tax structure were minor.[18] Probably the most essential provision of the 1958 constitutional amendment was the one which permitted the federal government to continue to levy its national defense income tax, its sales tax, and its beer tax until 1964.[19]

Unless there is a drastic reduction in the expenditures of the Swiss government, which does not seem likely, something further will have to be done by 1964. The income from the federal national defense income tax and the federal sales tax alone amounted to 1,497,552,000 Swiss francs in 1962, or almost half of the Confederation's total income for that year. However repugnant it may be to many Swiss, a permanent federal income tax appears to be inevitable.

[18] For instance, the Confederation's income from the military service exemption tax was increased.

[19] See *Arrêté fédéral instituant de nouvelles dispositions constitutionnelles sur le régime financier de la Confédération,* Jan. 31, 1958.

✠ *10* ✠

Neutrality and Foreign Policy

Neutrality is a word which is closely associated with Switzerland. For over four hundred years the country has made it a policy to remain aloof from the conflicts in which her European neighbors have been involved and to refuse offers of political or military alliance in peacetime. Moreover, for almost a century and a half the major world powers have recognized this policy and, with a few minor exceptions, have scrupulously respected it.

Neutrality, of course, does not signify the lack of a foreign policy. To the contrary, a country which has adopted such an attitude must have a dynamic foreign policy to enable it to carry out demanding tasks in both peace and war. Switzerland is in a particularly difficult position in this matter both because it is landlocked and because it depends chiefly on international trade for prosperity. World War II, for instance, was a supreme test of Swiss diplomatic skill.

Furthermore, Switzerland has interpreted neutrality as compatible with participation in the work of international organizations. The policy of staying out of political and military alliance yet cooperating in other international endeavors is given the popular title "neutrality and solidarity." It was a member of the League of Nations, and helped to organize many other international organizations with headquarters still on Swiss soil. Although not now a member of the United Nations, Switzerland has rendered many services to it, and its European headquarters are in Geneva.

This chapter deals with the overall foreign policy of Switzerland, including both the concept of neutrality and that of active participation in international affairs.

Neutrality

Origins

The true beginning of Swiss neutrality occurred in 1515 when the Swiss troops were soundly defeated by Francis I in the Battle of Marignano. In the preceding centuries, Switzerland had slowly built up a reputation as an important military power and its troops a reputation of invincibility. It had come to the point where one of the first actions of a country intent on war was to try to enlist the Swiss as allies. The Swiss were happy to oblige for proper consideration, such as payment for the services of its troops and a share in the spoils of war.

Although the Swiss performed at Marignano with their accustomed bravery, a combination of perfidious Swiss allies, well-disciplined French cavalry, and skillful artillery were too much for the Swiss infantry. The losses suffered raised grave doubts in the minds of the Swiss people as to the desirability of continuing their policy of imperialistic expansion. As a result, it was decided to forswear any future alliances except for defensive purposes. The Swiss did not go so far, however, as to forbid the recruiting of their mercenaries to fight in European armies.

Before the Swiss had an opportunity to change their attitude, they became preoccupied with internal problems resulting from the Reformation. Divided as the country was, with two more or less equal religious groups, Switzerland had to struggle to keep its own confederation intact. Not only was it too occupied to enter into outside alliances, but it would not have been an effective ally to anyone in its disorganized state.

Paralyzed as it was by its own religious problems, Switzerland did not participate in the Thirty Years War. At the start, the Swiss, fearing civil war, refused to answer calls for help from either side. Later it became apparent that neutrality had other benefits, saving Swiss territory from the ravages of war being the most important one. In the end, Swiss troops were used only to suppress internal disturbances and to prevent violation of Swiss territory by warring parties.

The nation continued its policy of neutrality during the succession of European wars in the seventeenth and eighteenth centuries. For a while Switzerland's neighbors looked suspiciously upon neutrality, and were kept at bay only by the readiness of the people to defend their borders forcefully. Soon, however, Swiss neutrality came to be considered as an asset. Both France and Austria, for example, looked with favor on a neutral Switzerland guarding their Alpine flanks and began making payments to keep it strong. In 1688 Switzerland went so far as to request and receive subsidies from both France and Austria, even though each knew that Switzerland was receiving aid from the other.[1]

While the outbreak of the French Revolution brought internal strife to Switzerland, there was at first no immediate threat to its territorial integrity. Later when the Coalition declared war on France, Switzerland declined invitations to participate, and declared her neutrality. France was especially pleased with the Swiss stand since it meant assurance of a source of food and war materials. In fact when their own resources ran low, the Swiss purchased necessary supplies in Swabia, Austria, Italy, and Hungary, and transshipped them to France.

With the end of the Austrian war, Swiss neutrality was no longer an asset to the French. Thus, in order to suppress reactionary activities in Switzerland and to open the Italian passes to French troops, the French invaded and conquered the Confederation in 1798. Forced to be allies of France, the Swiss again found themselves involved in foreign wars, a position which ended only with Napoleon's defeat.

Shaken by its recent experience with the French, and recalling the prosperous and relatively peaceful days preceding French intervention, the Swiss sent a delegate to the Congress of Vienna with express instructions to obtain international recognition of neutrality for the future.

Neutrality Recognized

The Swiss delegate to the 1815 Congress was successful in his mission. On March 20, the great powers assured Switzerland of their intention to recognize and guarantee her "perpetual neutrality." Further, in an act signed at Paris on November 20, 1815, Austria, France, Great Britain, Prussia, and Russia recognized "formally and authentically" the "perpetual neutrality of Switzerland" and "that the neutrality and integrity of Switzerland and her independence from any foreign influence are in the true interests of European policy as a whole."[2]

[1] W. E. Rappard, *Collective Security in Swiss Experience* (London: George Allen & Unwin, Ltd., 1948), pp. 118–124.

[2] See Rappard, *The Government of Switzerland*, pp. 132–133, and Bonjour and others, *A Short History of Switzerland*, p. 243. For a guide to Swiss literature on the question of whether the Congress of Vienna guaranteed Swiss neutrality or was merely a recognition thereof, see Jacqueline Belin, *La Suisse et les Nations Unies* (New York: Manhattan Publishing Co., 1956), p. 21, ftn. 14.

Switzerland had a few details to attend to herself before she could be said to have achieved a genuine position of neutrality. The most obvious discrepancy between neutrality in principle and neutrality in fact was the providing of Swiss mercenary troops on a contractual basis to foreign powers. The first step taken to settle the issue was Article 11 of the 1848 Constitution: "Military capitulations may not be concluded." The new Swiss government then brought to a conclusion, as rapidly as possible, the treaties by which the cantons supplied soldiers to other countries. Brooks places the last of the capitulation treaties at 1859, while Hughes states: "Recruitment of mercenaries by foreign powers under conditions often popularly called capitulations continued more or less openly into the 1870's."[3] The only remnants of the old mercenary system that exist at present are the Pope's Swiss Guard, not considered military service under the terms of the constitution, and the periodic enlistment of Swiss in the French Foreign Legion, although this is actually illegal under federal law.

Another provision of the 1848 Constitution to help make Switzerland as neutral as possible was Article 12 prohibiting "members of the federal authorities, civil or military officials of the confederation, and the representatives on federal commissions" from accepting any pension, salary, title, gift, or decoration from a foreign government. Those who had already received them from foreign governments, and there were many at the time, were permitted to undertake their functions only if they refused pensions, and did not wear decorations, during the terms of office. A later amendment included certain cantonal officials and all members of the military in the prohibition. This made it necessary to renounce completely any pension, to renounce the wearing of any decoration, or to return the decoration to the government which had granted it if one wished to serve in public office.[4]

Neutrality in Practice

Switzerland has had several occasions to test her neutrality, some of minor importance and some major. Among the former were the Franco-Sardinian War against Austria in 1859 and the Franco-Prussian War of 1870–71. The restricted nature of these conflicts did not pose any particular problem to Swiss diplomacy, although in the latter war there was considerable French sentiment on the part of the French-speaking population. As noted by Brooks, when the French army of General Bourbaki was driven over the border into Switzerland during

[3] See Brooks, *Government and Politics of Switzerland*, p. 278, and Hughes, *The Federal Constitution of Switzerland*, p. 13.

[4] Art. 12 of the 1874 Constitution as amended in 1931.

the Franco-Prussian War, "they disarmed it, interning officers and men, and caring for them with whole-hearted hospitality until the end of the war."[5]

Neutrality in World War I and World War II was much more difficult for the Swiss. In the first place, the scope of the conflict was much wider. In Europe, at least, Switzerland was one of a minority of countries not involved with either side in World War I. In World War II, Switzerland was one of a very small minority of the entire world not involved. In the second place, the nature of the conflicts differed from those that had occurred earlier. It was much more difficult especially in World War II, for Switzerland to maintain a personal, as opposed to an official, impartiality. The manner in which it carried out its self-imposed responsibilities, and some of the resulting problems, will be the subject of the remainder of this section.

At the outbreak of European hostilities in 1914, the Swiss government immediately issued a declaration of its intent not to depart in any way from "the principles of neutrality so dear to the Swiss people."[6] This was followed by the election of Ulrich Wille as Commander in Chief, the rapid mobilization of troops to guard the frontiers, and the conferring upon the Federal Council "full powers" to take the measures necessary to protect Switzerland's independence.

One of the first problems that confronted the Swiss government was to prevent an open display of partisanship in favor of the French or the Germans. The problem was especially grave in the French-speaking parts of Switzerland where, after the German attack on Belgium, the people were entirely in sympathy with France and Great Britain. In certain German-speaking areas, the cultural affinity with Germany and admiration of its industry also kept many Swiss on the German side. In the beginning, the government contented itself with exhortations to the people to remain true to the cause of Swiss neutrality, but later it imposed restrictions on the freedom of the press.

The second problem was the effect of war on the Swiss economy. Switzerland was dependent upon Germany for such basic items as coal and iron, upon the Allies for not only most other raw materials, but also for foodstuffs, and upon both for export markets. As the war continued, Switzerland came under severe Allied pressure to limit its German trade and a counter German pressure to continue the same trade. Through skillful and delicate maneuvering the Swiss government was able to satisfy both sides in the conflict and keep its economy at quite a high level. In fact, one observer of Swiss neutrality was able

[5] Brooks, p. 278.
[6] *Ibid.*, p. 279.

to state that the country "not only fared better than any belligerent but also derived more advantage than disadvantage, economically, from the war situation."[7]

The third problem was that of keeping government officials from acting in a way that could be considered by the belligerents as un-neutral. Two such incidents did occur in World War I, one involving two army officers and one a member of the Federal Council. The two officers, Colonel Karl Egli and Colonel Moritz von Wattenwyl, were accused and convicted of supplying the Austrian and German military attachés with copies of general staff bulletins concerning Allied troop movements. This incident caused extensive criticism abroad and at home, especially among the citizens of the French-speaking cantons.[8] The Federal Council member whose actions tended to compromise Swiss neutrality was Arthur Hoffmann, the head of the Federal Political Department. In June of 1917, Hoffmann's behavior was discovered to be such as to place him under suspicion of acting as an intermediary between the Central Powers and Russia in what was considered to be an attempt by the latter to negotiate a separate German peace. The storm of protest that followed this disclosure was calmed when Hoffmann resigned, and the Federal Assembly quickly elected another man to take his place on the Federal Council.

From a humanitarian point of view, Switzerland did much that was good during the conflict. In this she was aided by the facts that not only did she remain in contact with both belligerents throughout the war but also the country was split in its sympathies, with some for the Allies and some for the Central Powers. In the early stages many of her activities centered around the repatriation of foreign civilians caught within the national boundaries of one side or the other. Later she concentrated on the exchange of sick and wounded. With the agreement of the belligerents, Switzerland also began the task of caring for their sick prisoners of war. One authority places the total number of such individuals at 68,000 from 1916 to the end of the war.[9] The Swiss Government and the International Committee of the Red Cross also performed important duties, such as keeping lists of the dead and prisoners of war, and arranging for the exchange of packages and mail between the hostile prison camps.

[7] Traugott Geering, as quoted in Edgar Turlington, *The World War Period,* Volume III of *Neutrality, Its History, Economics and Law* (New York: Columbia University Press, 1936), p. 143. For a comprehensive account of Swiss economic relations with the Allies and the Central Powers during World War I, see pp. 132–143 of the same work.

[8] See George Soloveytchik, *Switzerland in Perspective* (London: Oxford University Press, 1954), p. 223.

[9] See Bonjour and others, *A Short History of Switzerland,* p. 354.

Neutrality in World War II

With the outbreak of hostilities in 1939, Switzerland again issued her neutrality declaration and began the mobilization of her economic and military resources. Trade was to continue with the warring powers, but on a basis of strict impartiality. As before, there were sympathies for France in the French-speaking cantons and a certain amount of pro-German activity in other areas that had to be kept within bounds. For a while it was expected that the situation would develop as it had during World War I.

With the fall of France in 1940, however, the situation changed completely. No longer was Switzerland a neutral between two hostile powers; it had become a neutral state completely surrounded by the forces of only one of the belligerents. This development forced several changes in Swiss policy. The attempt to defend all the frontiers, for instance, was abandoned, and Swiss defenses were centered around the Alpine fortifications. Special measures were taken to utilize all possible land for the production of food, and laws were passed to control prices and rents.

There was also a change in the people's attitude. When the German intentions became known, there was a noticeable lack of German sympathizers. When France established the Vichy government, sympathy for France was likewise absent. Despite repeated declarations by the government that neutrality was a state affair and that the individual was free to think as he pleased, the Swiss government took severe measures to assure that Switzerland's neutrality would not be compromised: first, the Communist and Nazi front parties were outlawed, and second, harsh penalties were provided for any propaganda contrary to the Swiss neutral spirit.

The Swiss economy became almost entirely subject to the whims of the Axis powers. Trade, on which the economy depended, had to be carried on with the Axis or through the territory controlled by their powers. As a consequence, the amount of Switzerland's trade with the Axis rose as trade with the Allies fell. Despite handicaps, however, the Swiss continued throughout the war to maintain economic relations with the Allies and to deliver goods to them. Many of these goods passed through Italy by way of the port of Genoa.

Notwithstanding Switzerland's precarious position, she was not exempt from Allied pressures to curtail her Axis trade as much as possible. In 1939 and 1940 the Allies demanded that she participate in the blockade of Germany. In 1943 London and Washington requested that Switzerland refuse to transship petroleum across her territory. In 1944 they requested a further reduction in transport of goods between

Germany and Italy. It is a fact that the Swiss did do all in their power to restrict trade to goods not classified as war material. It is also a fact that Switzerland remained throughout the war a vital supply link between Germany and Italy. Although the Allies' official policy toward Switzerland was not completely cordial, much sympathy for the Swiss existed on an unofficial basis. One of the best evidences of this is the note from Winston Churchill to the British Foreign Secretary in December, 1944, part of which reads:

> I put this down for record. Of all the neutrals Switzerland has the greatest right to distinction. She has been the sole international force linking the hideously sundered nations and ourselves. What does it matter whether she has been able to give us the commercial advantages we desire or has given too many to the Germans, to keep herself alive? She has been a democratic State, standing for freedom in self-defense among her mountains, and in thought, in spite of race, largely on our side.[10]

No one, of course, would take issue with the humanitarian activities undertaken in Switzerland during World War II. Over two hundred thousand refugees were received despite the small size of the country and warnings from the government about overcrowding. Several hundreds of millions of Swiss francs were donated by the federal government, the cantonal governments, and private individuals to be used to aid war victims in some seventeen European countries. The Central Prisoner of War Agency, used to such good effect in World War I, was re-established by the Red Cross Committee and managed to transmit almost 120 million messages to war prisoners or their families.[11]

After the war, Switzerland was able to re-establish normal relations with other states despite a certain degree of resentment over her wartime neutrality. After some negotiation, for instance, she agreed to turn over to the Allies half of the German assets that had been in Swiss safekeeping during the war. The United States, on the other hand, unblocked most of the Swiss funds it had frozen at the onset of the war. Notwithstanding a violent denunciation of Switzerland and her policies in 1944, in 1946 the U.S.S.R. resumed the diplomatic relations that had been interrupted some thirty years earlier.

The material that follows will deal with the Swiss diplomatic establishment and some of the problems that have confronted the Swiss during the inter-war years and since the end of World War II.

[10] Winston S. Churchill, *Triumph and Tragedy* (Boston: Houghton Mifflin Company, 1953), p. 712.

[11] Denis de Rougemont, *La Confédération helvétique* (Monaco: Rocher, 1953), p. 174.

Diplomatic and Consular Service

While the general conduct of Swiss foreign affairs is vested in the Federal Council as a body, direct responsibility is entrusted to the Political Department and the Federal Councillor at its head. The Political Department makes regular reports to the Federal Council on important political events that take place in the world, it conducts negotiations with foreign governments, and it assures the protection of Swiss citizens and Swiss interests abroad. To aid it in these tasks, the Political Department has a wide network of embassies, legations, and consulates throughout the world. The increasing involvement of Switzerland in international affairs is nowhere better reflected than in the changes that have taken place in the diplomatic and consular services over the past hundred years.

For many years after the creation of the federal government, the Swiss were content to keep only a very modest diplomatic establishment. Until late in the nineteenth century, Switzerland limited its diplomatic representation to its immediate neighbors, Austria, France, Germany, and Italy. A legation in Washington was added in 1882, one in London and one in Buenos Aires in 1891. This last was in charge of Swiss diplomatic relations with four countries: Argentina, Chile, Paraguay, and Uruguay. Swiss relations with other countries were carried out through Swiss consulates or the good offices of the United States and Germany. For a long time, American diplomatic agents protected Swiss citizens and interests in Latin America with the exception of the aforementioned countries.[12]

The two World Wars created a tremendously heavy burden for the Swiss diplomatic missions. At the outbreak of World War I, neutral states, including Switzerland, assumed control of the belligerents' interests in enemy territory. When the United States changed from neutral status to belligerent in 1917, its charges were turned over to the remaining neutrals, with Switzerland taking a large share. The process was repeated in World War II. This time, because there were many fewer neutrals, Switzerland became the diplomatic caretaker for almost the entire world. Denis de Rougemont estimates that during the period 1939 to 1945 Switzerland agreed to defend the interests of some forty-three belligerent states on the territory of their enemies.[13]

Among the tasks undertaken by Swiss diplomatic officials for their clients during wartime were: safeguarding official property left be-

[12] Carl Charlick, "Diplomatic Caretaker," *Foreign Service Journal,* **32** (October, 1955), 22.

[13] De Rougemont, p. 176.

hind, such as buildings and records; safeguarding, or negotiating the release of private property left behind by the official staffs; and negotiating, wherever possible, the repatriation of private citizens. Where it was impossible to achieve repatriation, the Swiss arranged for their protection, which included making relief payments to those who fell destitute as a result of losing their means of livelihood. Where enemy aliens were interned, especially in the Far East, the Swiss diplomatic personnel made every attempt to obtain humane treatment for them. Another demanding task was to arrange for the exchange of diplomatic personnel, families, and staffs. In the spring of 1942, for example, the Swiss negotiated the exchange of some 1,800 Allied and Axis diplomatic personnel through neutral Lisbon and, in 1943, the exchange of 6,600 persons to and from the Far East. In each case the Swiss not only made arrangements to assure the vessels involved of safe passage through war zones but also sent foreign service officers to accompany each group to the point of embarkation.[14] All of these activities were added to their own large-scale humanitarian works on Swiss soil.

To meet its increasing responsibilities over the years, the country has strengthened and enlarged its diplomatic representation. The dozen Swiss diplomatic establishments existing prior to World War I were increased to thirty-two by 1939, and fifty-three in 1958. Further, in 1956 the Federal Council was given permission to elevate its legations to embassies. Before 1956 the highest diplomatic envoy in the Swiss foreign service was a Minister. This was noteworthy, especially in France, which had for many years previously sent an Ambassador to Berne. By 1960 forty-one Swiss legations had been elevated to embassies. With these, fourteen ministries, and more than one hundred consulates, the Swiss diplomatic and consular service is now in a position to undertake almost any task that might be entrusted to it.

International Organizations

Switzerland has a long record of participation in international organizations. In 1865 she was one of the founders of the International Telegraph Union in Paris, the permanent bureau of which was opened in 1869 at Berne. In 1936 it became the International Telecommunication Union and by a decision made in 1947 the headquarters were shifted from Berne to Geneva. The second oldest of the truly international organizations, the Universal Postal Union, was created by a conference at Berne in October, 1874. Berne was also chosen for the location of its permanent office which began operations in September, 1875. Among the other international organizations appearing on Swiss soil in the nineteenth century, one should mention the International

[14] Charlick, p. 42.

Red Cross Committee created in 1864, the International Railway Transport Office founded in 1893, and the International Bureau of Industrial Property established in 1888. In each case the Swiss government was given the duty of supervising the overall work of the organ, controlling its finances, and staffing it with Swiss citizens.[15]

After considerable soul-searching, Switzerland also became an active member of the League of Nations. Doubts were expressed over the possible incompatibility of neutrality with the concept of collective security to which the League was dedicated. As stated by Professor Guggenheim, noted Swiss professor of international law: "The State which is pledged on the one hand to neutrality, on the other to participation in collective security, is thus confronted with the problem of a genuine conflict of duties. It cannot at one and the same time fulfill two contrary obligations, and must therefore necessarily infringe one or the other."[16]

The solution arrived at was a compromise of both principles. On the one hand, Switzerland agreed to participate in economic sanctions against any state that the League should deem to be an aggressor. On the other hand, Switzerland was specifically exempt, in deference to her policy of neutrality, from engaging in any military action decided upon by the League or from permitting free passage of foreign troops across her territory. Three months after this League agreement, the government put the question of joining the organization to the people in referendum. On May 16, 1920, the Swiss agreed to join by a vote of 416,870 to 323,719. There was a majority in favor in ten cantons and three half-cantons, and a majority against in nine cantons and three half-cantons.

Switzerland was an active member during the League's short existence. It also willingly acceded to the obligatory jurisdiction clause of the Permanent International Court of Justice statutes. It was chosen as the site for headquarters not only of the League as a whole but also of the International Labor Organization.

As long as the League remained a center for the dissemination of information and a forum for the discussion of international issues, Switzerland found no reason to regret its membership. The Italo-Ethiopian conflict was another matter. The Swiss were called upon, along with the other members of the League, to impose economic sanctions on Italy. Since Italy was a close neighbor, it was a real test of

---

[15] When the International Telecommunication Union and the Universal Postal Union became Specialized Agencies of the United Nations after World War II, their staffs were internationalized.

[16] As quoted in Walter Hofer, *Neutrality as the Principle of Swiss Foreign Policy* (Zurich: Schweizer Spiegel Verlag, 1957), p. 15.

Switzerland's good faith. For a while Switzerland remained true to its obligations and did attempt to apply certain restrictions. Finally, however, they applied to the League for release from their commitments which, as the Swiss delegate explained, were becoming a threat to her very existence. On May 11, 1938, the Council of the League stated that it "takes cognizance of Switzerland's intention not to participate henceforth in any way in the application of sanctions provided for by the Covenant, and declares that she shall no longer be called upon to do so."[17] As a result, the nation retreated to its policy of "integral neutrality."[18]

So far, Switzerland has not become a member of the United Nations nor has it even submitted an application to join. The major reason given is that the United Nations system of collective security is incompatible with Switzerland's traditional neutrality. The Swiss have no intention of giving up their neutrality until they are certain that the collective security system is workable. Furthermore, they, as do the people of many another small country, do not like the provisions for the five-power veto in the Security Council. They feel that no nation, despite its relative power, should be able to block collective security measures. Furthermore, no large popular sentiment in favor of joining the United Nations exists in the country. Of the three major political parties, only the Socialists advocate such an action.

There is reason to believe, however, that Switzerland would have joined the organization immediately after World War II, as it did the League of Nations after World War I. When it first came to their attention, the Swiss were receptive to the idea of creating a new international organization, and they sent an observer, Professor Rappard, to the San Francisco Conferences. As late as 1946 the Federal Council published a statement in which it expressed the opinion that a country "which played a role in the League of Nations and which continues to do so in international organization, cannot remain indifferent to the United Nations."[19] Most official pronouncements also carried some mention of Switzerland's neutrality. There is no reason to believe that Switzerland would not also have joined the United Nations if she had been invited and if some concessions had been made to her neutrality. However, no invitations were forthcoming. To the contrary, statements were made on several occasions by members that the United Nations system was completely incompatible with any form of neutrality.

Nevertheless, Switzerland has made an important contribution, and

[17] As quoted in Hofer, p. 18.
[18] For a detailed discussion of the activities of Switzerland in the League of Nations, see Belin, *La Suisse et les Nations Unies,* pp. 39–57.
[19] Belin, p. 73.

continues to do so, to the United Nations system. First of all, the UN's European Headquarters are located at Geneva in the old League buildings. The country has also become a member of not only the International Court of Justice but also the International Opium Commission and the Permanent Central Opium Board, the last two mentioned being under the authority of the United Nations Economic and Social Council. It also contributes heavily to the United Nations' International Children's Emergency Fund. Furthermore, it provided one of the Neutral Commissions charged with the exchange of prisoners at the cessation of the United Nations action in Korea. In addition, Switzerland is an active member of many of the United Nations Specialized Agencies, such as the Food and Agriculture Organization, General Agreement on Tariffs and Trade, the International Civil Aviation Organization, UNESCO, the World Health Organization, and the World Meteorological Organization. The headquarters of the two latter agencies are located in Geneva. Switzerland has provided a United Nations High Commission for Refugees and it continues its membership in the three oldest Specialized Agencies: the International Labor Organization, the International Telecommunication Union, and the Universal Postal Union. Each of these has had its headquarters in Switzerland since its inception. Although not a member of the World Bank, Switzerland has made considerable capital available to it. "From 1951 to 1960, eight World Bank loans totalling 460 million Swiss francs were issued in the Swiss market. In 1957 the federal government moreover granted the Bank a loan of 200 million francs. Together these 660 million francs amounted to about six times the cash quota Switzerland would have to contribute to become a member of the World Bank."[20]

Switzerland has also been active in the channeling of aid to the underdeveloped countries of the world. Financial support to the technical assistance programs of the United Nations and its Specialized Agencies totalled about one million francs annually from 1951 to 1956, one and a half million in 1957 and 1958, and three and a half million in 1959. The Federal Assembly has voted to increase this amount to four million francs annually from 1960 to 1962. Some two hundred Swiss nationals were sent on missions to underdeveloped countries from 1950 to 1959, including the Congo; and, in the same period, Switzerland has received 780 individuals from the underdeveloped countries. Furthermore, Swiss direct private investment in the world's underdeveloped areas is one of the highest per capita in Western Europe. The conclusion seems to be obvious that whether or not

[20] Rudolf Frei, "Swiss Aid to Underdeveloped Countries," *Swiss Review of World Affairs,* X (October, 1960), 10.

Switzerland becomes a member of the United Nations, it is making an important contribution to its work.

European Economic Integration

The movement toward European economic integration poses a special problem for the Swiss. Switzerland's prosperity is dependent on the ability to buy and sell goods with the other countries of Europe, especially her close neighbors. Any discrimination against Swiss goods, either by inadvertence or by design, can have serious consequences for the Swiss economy. The country, therefore, must do all in its power to keep the European economy as strong and free as possible.

In keeping with this policy, Switzerland in 1948 became a member of the Organization for European Economic Cooperation (OEEC). The purpose of the OEEC was to restore the conditions necessary for free European trade, particularly that of the free convertibility of money. The Swiss made it plain that they did not want any of the American gifts or loans under the Marshall Plan but only wanted to help restore Europe to a prosperous trading area.[21] Switzerland also has joined the European Payments Union.[22]

The Swiss regarded the creation of the European Common Market by France, Germany, Italy, and the Benelux countries as a different matter, however. In the first place, it had political overtones that were repugnant to them. They would not join. Many thought of the European Common Market as a means for creating close political ties between the six member countries, and perhaps for creating a single nation in the future. If nothing else, real economic integration of the six countries could be achieved only with a greater degree of political solidarity than had existed before. Switzerland has always made it a policy to stay away from any organization with such overtones, such as the Council of Europe. As stated by Willy Bretscher, editor of the *Neue Zürcher Zeitung:* "Joining a structure designed to evolve into a European superstate, would in the case of Switzerland, a neutral small nation, imply abandoning essential parts of its national sovereignty, with the result of a real danger to its political independence, its neutrality, its federative structure, and its democratic way of life."[23]

---

[21] Switzerland has become a member of the Organization for Economic Cooperation and Development (OECD) which has replaced the OEEC.

[22] Switzerland is also a member of the European Committee for Nuclear Research.

[23] Willy Bretscher, "Switzerland and European Integration," *Swiss Review of World Affairs,* X (April, 1960), 2.

In the second place, the European Common Market as created without Swiss participation poses a threat to the Swiss economy. The proposed tariff reductions among the members would, if enacted, place Switzerland in a disadvantageous position. A large percentage of Swiss trade has always been with France and Germany and to a certain extent with Italy. Thus, any other economic measures contemplated by the European Common Market, such as quantitative trade restrictions, would further harm Swiss trade.

Switzerland first joined with other countries outside of the Common Market to try to negotiate a larger European free trade area to include most of the OEEC countries. After a breakdown in the negotiations, seven countries — Austria, Denmark, Great Britain, Norway, Portugal, Sweden, and Switzerland — then joined in a "protective alliance" known as the European Free-Trade Association. The purpose of the new Association was not only to protect its members from discriminatory measures taken by the Common Market, but also to pressure the Common Market countries to retain free European trade. As explained by Mr. Bretscher:

> The EFTA is certainly not an ideal solution. But under the given conditions it is the best possible solution in a distinctly critical situation. Switzerland's joining it is this country's contribution to the economic integration of Europe. Switzerland thereby commits itself to a philosophy of integration that does not allow any of the current conflicting doctrines and methods of European cooperation or association to claim exclusivity, but, opposing any forced coordination, upholds the principle of free cooperation among the various forms and methods as the right way to strengthen the whole of Europe. Switzerland thus stands for an idea of a future Europe in which the individuality of every state, as evolved in the course of history, is preserved and the vital diversity of large, small and smallest communities on the old continent can continue to have its place within the framework of unity that is aimed at.[24]

Switzerland and Liechtenstein

Before concluding this chapter, mention should be made of the relationship between Liechtenstein and Switzerland. Liechtenstein is a small principality situated on the Eastern border of Switzerland with some fifteen to twenty thousand inhabitants. It had received its independence in 1806 at the time of the break-up of the Holy Roman Empire and in 1852 concluded a treaty with Austria bringing it into the Austro-Hungarian customs union. After the dissolution of the

[24] *Ibid.*, 3.

Austro-Hungarian nation immediately after World War I, the Prince of Liechtenstein petitioned for a similar arrangement with Switzerland. The Swiss accepted and by a series of treaties beginning in 1920 have made Liechtenstein practically a protectorate of Switzerland similar in many ways to the dependent territories that existed during the days of the Old Confederation.

In the first treaty, concluded on November 10, 1920, the Swiss agreed to incorporate Liechtenstein's postal, telephone, and telegraph systems into its own. In March, 1923, a further agreement was negotiated in which Switzerland added the collecting of customs to the duties it undertook for the principality. The customs agreement included much more, however. All duties between the two countries were abolished and the Swiss set up their control points on the further frontier of Liechtenstein. In payment for the loss of tariffs, the Swiss agreed to grant an annual sum of 150,000 Swiss francs to the Liechtenstein treasury. The amount was increased to 250,000 francs in 1926 and in 1950 the agreement was changed to an annual percentage of customs receipts after the deduction of a yearly sum to cover the costs of administration. Other results of the 1923 agreement include the use of Swiss money as the legal tender in Liechtenstein, the imposition by Liechtenstein of many Swiss laws such as those concerning counterfeiting of bank notes, the forbidding of absinthe production, the agreement not to open gambling houses, and the application of Swiss laws on patents and copyrights.

The Swiss have taken over the diplomatic representation of Liechtenstein and the defense of its interests with regard to foreign nations. Switzerland has been given control over the movement of foreigners within Liechtenstein. About the only area in which the principality retains its "sovereignty" is in relation to the administration of justice. Even there, however, the principality has agreed to adapt the Swiss Civil Code for local use and in fact several members of the higher courts in Liechtenstein are Swiss citizens. As described by Professor Sauser-Hall, with the conclusion of the 1923 customs agreement, "the juridical situation of the principality, from the economic point of view, is analogous to that of a Swiss canton."[25] From a "neutral point of view," it looks as though Liechtenstein has actually become a Swiss canton in all respects except, perhaps, for the right of the principality to issue its own postage stamps.

[25] Sauser-Hall, *Guide politique suisse*, p. 272. It should also be noted that the agreement is valid for a five-year term, renewable by tacit agreement.

ANNEX

Electoral Systems for Cantonal Executive and Legislative Bodies

(Status on May 31, 1963)*

Canton	Executive			Legislative		
	Number of Members	Method of Election	Method of Election of President	Number of Members	Length of Term	Electoral System
Zurich	7	U	R	180	4	P
Berne	9	U	V	200	4	P
Lucerne	7	U	V	170	4	P
Uri	7	U	U	54	4	M
Schwyz	7	U	V	105	4	P
Obwalden	7	L	L	38	4	M
Nidwalden	9	L	L	60	4	M
Glarus	7	L	L	81	3	M & P
Zug	7	U	V	78	4	P
Fribourg	7	U	V	130	5	P
Solothurn	5	U	R	144	4	P
Basle Town	7	U	V	130	4	P
Basle Country	5	U	V	80	4	P
Schaffhausen	5	U	V	82	4	P
Appenzell-Outer Rhodes	7	L	L	61	3	M
Appenzell-Inner Rhodes	9	L	L	60	1	M
St. Gallen	7	U	V	193	4	P
Grisons	5	U	V	113	2	M
Aargau	5	U	R	200	4	P
Thurgau	5	U	V	125	3	P
Tincino	5	U	R	65	4	P
Vaud	7	U	R	197	4	P
Valais	5	U	R	130	4	P
Neuchâtel	5	U	R	115	4	P
Geneva	7	U	R	100	4	P

U = By popular secret ballot
L = By the Landesgemeinde
R = The executive body elects its own President

V = By the cantonal legislative body
M = Majority
P = Proportional

Annuaire statistique 1963, p. 534.

SELECTED BIBLIOGRAPHY

DOCUMENTS

Annuaire statistique de la Suisse (Statistisches Jahrbuch der Schweiz). Official statistical information. Published since 1891.

Bulletin sténographique officiel de l'Assemblée fédérale suisse (Amtliches stenographisches Bulletin der schweizerischen Bundesversammlung). Debates in the Federal Assembly. Published since 1891.

Feuille fédérale de la Confédération Suisse (Bundesblatt der schweizerischen Eidgenossenschaft). Messages of Federal Council to the Federal Assembly, legislative committee reports, etc. Published since 1848.

Recueil officiel des lois et arrêtés fédéraux de la Confédération Suisse (Amtliche Sammlung der Bundesgesetze und Verordnungen der schweizerischen Eidgenossenschaft). Compilation of federal statutes and ordinances. Published since 1848.

GENERAL LITERATURE

Belin, Jacqueline. *La Suisse et les Nations Unies* (under the direction of Paul Guggenheim). New York: Manhattan Publishing Company, 1956.

Biaudet, Jean-Charles. *Les origines de la Constitution fédérale de 1848*. Lausanne: Publications de l'Université de Lausanne, 1949.

Bonjour, Edgar. *Geschichte der schweizerischen Neutralität, drei Jahrhunderte eidgenössischer Aussenpolitik*. Basel: Helbing und Lichtenhahn, 1946.

——, *Die Gründung des Schweizerischen Bundestaates*. Basel: B. Schwabe, 1948.

——, *Die Schweiz und Europa*. Basel: Helbing und Lichtenhahn, 1958.

——, *Swiss Neutrality: Its History and Meaning*. London: George Allen & Unwin Ltd., 1946.

Bonjour, E., H. S. Offler, and G. R. Potter. *A Short History of Switzerland*. London: Oxford University Press, 1952.

Bridel, Marcel. *L'ésprit et la destinée de la Constitution fédérale de 1848*. Lausanne: Publications de l'Université de Lausanne, 1949.

——, *Précis de droit constitutionnel et public suisse*. 2ème Partie, *Les organes de l'État*. Lausanne: Payot, 1959.

Brooks, Robert C. *Civic Training in Switzerland*. Chicago: University of Chicago Press, 1930.

——, *Government and Politics of Switzerland*. New York: World Book Company, 1921.

Brown, John M., "Switzerland," pp. 373–395 in *Foreign Governments: The Dynamics of Politics Abroad*, 2d ed., ed. Fritz Morstein Marx. New York: Prentice-Hall, 1952.

Bryce, James. *Modern Democracies*. 2 vols. New York: The Macmillan Company, 1921.

Burckhardt, Walter. *Kommentar der schweizerischen Bundesverfassung vom 29 Mai 1874*. 3. Auflage. Berne: Stampfli und Cie., 1931.

Deonna, Raymond. *Mémento de l'économie suisse*. Geneva: Les Éditions Radar, 1953.

Fleiner, Fritz and Zaccaria Giacometti. *Schweizerisches Bundesstaatsrecht*. Zurich: Polygraphischer Verlag AG., 1949.

Friedrich, Carl J., and Taylor Cole. *Responsible Bureaucracy: A Study of the Swiss Civil Service.* Cambridge, 1932.

Fueter, Eduard. *Die Schweiz seit 1848, Geschichte, Politik, Wirtschaft.* Zurich: O. Füssli Verlag, 1928.

Gafner, Raymond. *L'exercice du pouvoir fédéral par les autorités de la Confédération Suisse.* Lausanne: F. Roth Cie., 1945.

Gilliard, Charles. *A History of Switzerland.* London: George Allen & Unwin Ltd., 1955.

Herold, J. Christopher. *The Swiss Without Halos.* New York: Columbia University Press, 1948.

Hofer, Walther. *Neutrality as the Principle of Swiss Foreign Policy.* Zurich: Schweizer Spiegel Verlag, 1957.

Huber, Hans. *How Switzerland is Governed.* Zurich: Schweizer Spiegel Verlag, 1946.

Hughes, Christopher. *The Federal Constitution of Switzerland.* Oxford: Clarendon Press, 1954.

———, *The Parliament of Switzerland,* London: Oxford University Press, 1963.

Kohn, Hans. *Nationalism and Liberty: The Swiss Example.* London: George Allen & Unwin Ltd., 1956.

Lloyd, William B., Jr. *Waging Peace: The Swiss Experience.* Washington, D.C.: Public Affairs Press, 1958.

Meylan, René. *Géographie économique de la Suisse.* Lausanne: Payot, 1951.

Rappard, William E. *Cinq siècles de sécurité collective (1291–1798).* Geneva: Librairie Georg & Cie., 1945.

———, *Collective Security in Swiss Experience (1291–1948).* London: George Allen & Unwin Ltd., 1948.

———, *Les conditions de la prospérité helvétique.* Zurich: Buchdruckerei Berichthaus, 1957.

———, *La Constitution fédérale de la Suisse.* Neuchâtel: A la Baconnière, 1948.

———, *The Government of Switzerland.* New York: D. Van Nostrand Company, 1936.

———, *L'Individu et l'État dans l'évolution constitutionnelle de la Suisse.* Zurich: Éditions Polygraphiques, 1936.

Rappard, W. E. and others. *Source Book of European Governments.* New York: D. Van Nostrand Company, 1937.

Rice, William G. *Law Among States in Federacy.* Appleton, Wisconsin: C. C. Nelson Publishing Company, 1959.

de Rougemont, Denis. *La Confédération helvétique.* Monaco: Éditions du Rocher, 1953.

———, *Mission ou démission de la Suisse.* Neuchâtel: Éditions de la Baconnière, 1940.

de Rougemont, Denis and Charlotte Muret. *The Heart of Europe.* New York: Duell, Sloan and Pearce, 1941.

Ruffieux, Roland. "La Suisse contemporaine: état des travaux," *Revue française de sciences politique,* X (1960), 146–177.

Sauser-Hall, Georges. *Guide politique suisse.* Lausanne: Payot, 1956.

———, *The Political Institutions of Switzerland.* Zurich: Swiss National Tourist Office, 1946.

Siegfried, André. *La Suisse: Démocratie témoin,* 3d ed. Neuchâtel: A la Baconnière, 1956.

———, Switzerland: *A Democratic Way of Life.* New York: Duell, Sloan and Pearce, 1950. (English edition of *La Suisse: Démocratie témoin.*)

Soloveytchik, George. *Switzerland in Perspective.* London: Oxford University Press, 1954.

Spiro, Herbert J. *Government by Constitution.* New York: Random House, 1959.

Steiger, V. J. *Développement, principes et application de la législation sur l'alcool en Suisse.* (*La Question de l'alcool en Suisse, Cahier 25.*) Basel: Schwabe, 1954.

Steinmann, Ernst. *Geschichte des schweizerischen Freisinns.* Berne: Verlag P. Haupt, 1955.

Switzerland, Chancellerie fédérale. *Annuaire de la Confédération suisse, 1958.* (*Staatskalender der Schweizerischen Eidgenossenschaft.*) Berne, 1958.

———, ———, *Code pénal suisse* (*du 21 décembre 1937*). Berne, 1957.

———, ———, *Procédure fédérale: Organisation judiciaire, procédure civile, procédure pénale.* Berne, 1954.

———, Office fédéral de l'industrie, des arts et metiers et du travail. *Legislation sociale de la Suisse* (*Schweizerische Sozialgesetzgebung*). Zurich: Éditions Polygraphiques, 1959.

———, Secrétariat de l'Assemblée fédérale. *Membres des Chambres et du Conseil Fédéral, 36eme legislature.* Berne: 1960.

Tripp, M. L. *The Swiss and United States Federal Constitutional Systems* (Zurich thesis). Paris: 1940.

Turlington, Edgar. *The World War Period.* Vol. III of *Neutrality, Its History, Economics and Law.* New York: Columbia University Press, 1936.

Vergotti, Jacques M. *La Neutralité de la Suisse.* Lausanne: La Concorde, 1954.

de Weck, René. *La Suisse parmi les nations.* Geneva: Les Éditions du Cheval Ailé, 1946.

Wheare, K. C. *Federal Government.* London: Oxford University Press, 1946.

———, *Modern Constitutions.* London: Oxford University Press, 1951.

Zurcher, Arnold J. "The Political System of Switzerland," pp. 331–386 in *Governments of Continental Europe,* ed. James T. Shotwell. Rev. ed. New York: The Macmillan Company, 1952.

PERIODICALS

Gazette de Lausanne   *Neue Zürcher Zeitung*

Journal de Genève   *Swiss Review of World Affairs*

INDEX

A B C D E F G H I J – R – 7 3 2 1 0 / 6 9 8 7 6 5 4